CROMFORD & HIGH PEAK

by RAIL and TRAIL

Vic Mitchell & Keith Smith

Front cover: Then and now:-

Left: Pausing for a rest at Parsley Hay on 18th January 1967 is a regular worker, an 0-6-0ST with shining smokebox hinges. (J.R.Newman/Colour-Rail.com)

Right: The steam-powered winding house at Middleton Top is seen on 28th July 2016. The Trail passes it and the track fragments on the right. (P.G.Barnes)

Back cover: The solid black line indicates most of the route of this album. It is enlarged below the index, in map I.

Published October 2019

ISBN 978 1 910356 35 7

© Middleton Press Ltd, 2019

Production & Cover design Deborah Esher
Typesetting & Design Cassandra Morgan

Published by
    Middleton Press
    Easebourne Lane
    Midhurst
    West Sussex
    GU29 9AZ
Tel: 01730 813169
Email: info@middletonpress.co.uk
www.middletonpress.co.uk

Printed and bound by CPI Group (UK) Ltd, Croydon, CR0 4YY

INDEX

4	Cromford Wharf	56	Longcliffe Goods
67	Friden	32	Middleton
92	Grin Branch	60	Minninglow
89	Harpur Hill	73	Parsley Hay
1	High Peak Junction	102	Shallcross
87	Hindlow	17	Sheep Pasture
44	Hopton	108	Steeple Grange Light Railway
80	Hurdlow	30	Steeplehouse
94	Ladmanlow	103	Whaley Bridge

ACKNOWLEDGEMENTS

We are very grateful for the assistance received from many of those mentioned in the credits, also from J.M.Bentley, A.J.Castledine, G.Croughton, G.Gartside, J.Hinson (Signalling Record Society), C.M.Howard, N.Langridge, B.Lewis, the Steeple Grange Light Railway and, in particular, our always supportive families.

I. Our journey starts in the lower right corner and we run on the bold black line. The route running between DERBY and SHIRE is in our *Ambergate to Buxton* album. The Peak Forest Tramway is top left; see key. It was opened in 1799 and worked until 1923. In 1846, the Peak Forest Canal and Tramway had both passed into the ownership of the Sheffield, Ashton-under-Lyne & Manchester Railway. It was soon to be a constituent of the Manchester, Sheffield & Lincolnshire and later the ambitious Great Central Railway, after when it was owned by the London & North Eastern Railway. Closure was in about 1926.
(*The Railway Magazine*, 1934)

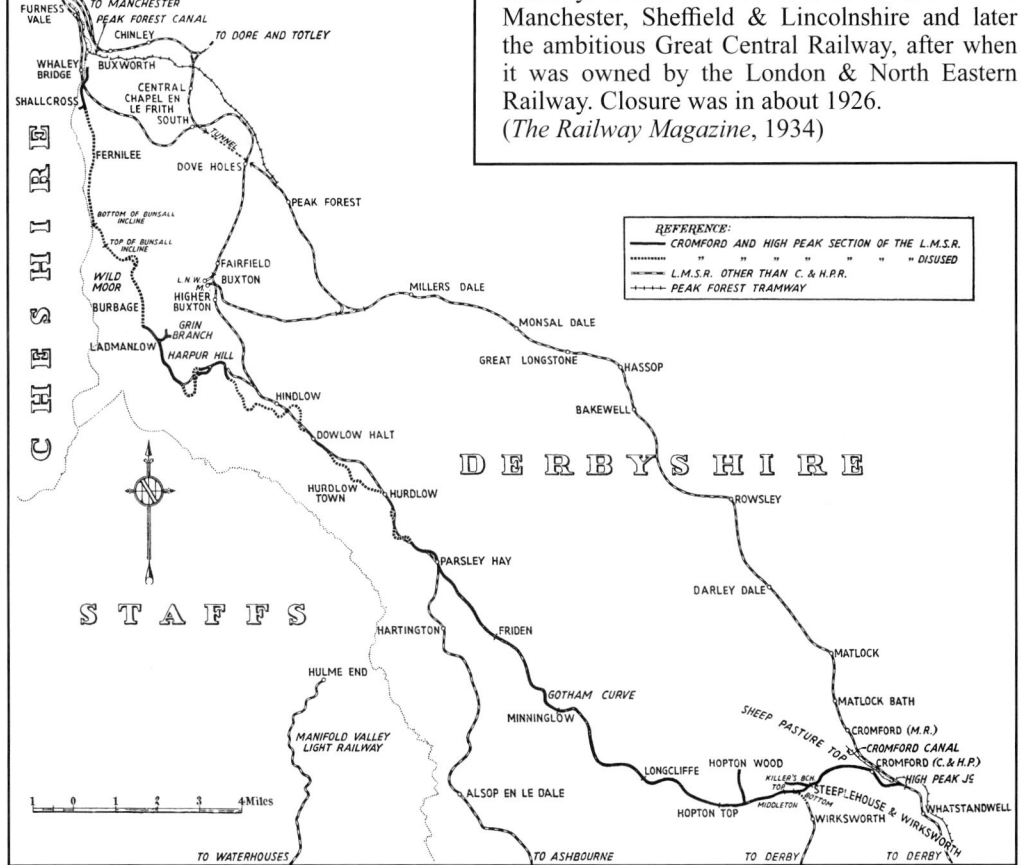

GEOGRAPHICAL SETTING

The Peak District is the highest part of the Pennine Hills, which run north-south and separated the developing industrial areas of the North of England. The relevant counties are revealed on map I, but the canals are not. They developed each side of the Pennines, but they were too high to be crossed without reservoirs to supply the locks.

The hills were composed extensively of limestone, which was quarried widely in this area until the 1970s. The rivers in the valleys were once an important source of power. This initiated many important industries and the district is known by geologists as the Derbyshire Dome. It contains much sandstone used for building and for grinding purposes.

The land formations necessitated the provision of many tunnels and rope-hauled inclines, worked by stationary steam engines. The local lead mines were once numerous, but were largely worked out by the time of rail transport. Few need to be told of the scenic attractions that have brought so many visitors over most of three centuries, war times excluded.

The other maps are scaled at 25ins to 1 mile, with north at the top, unless otherwise indicated.

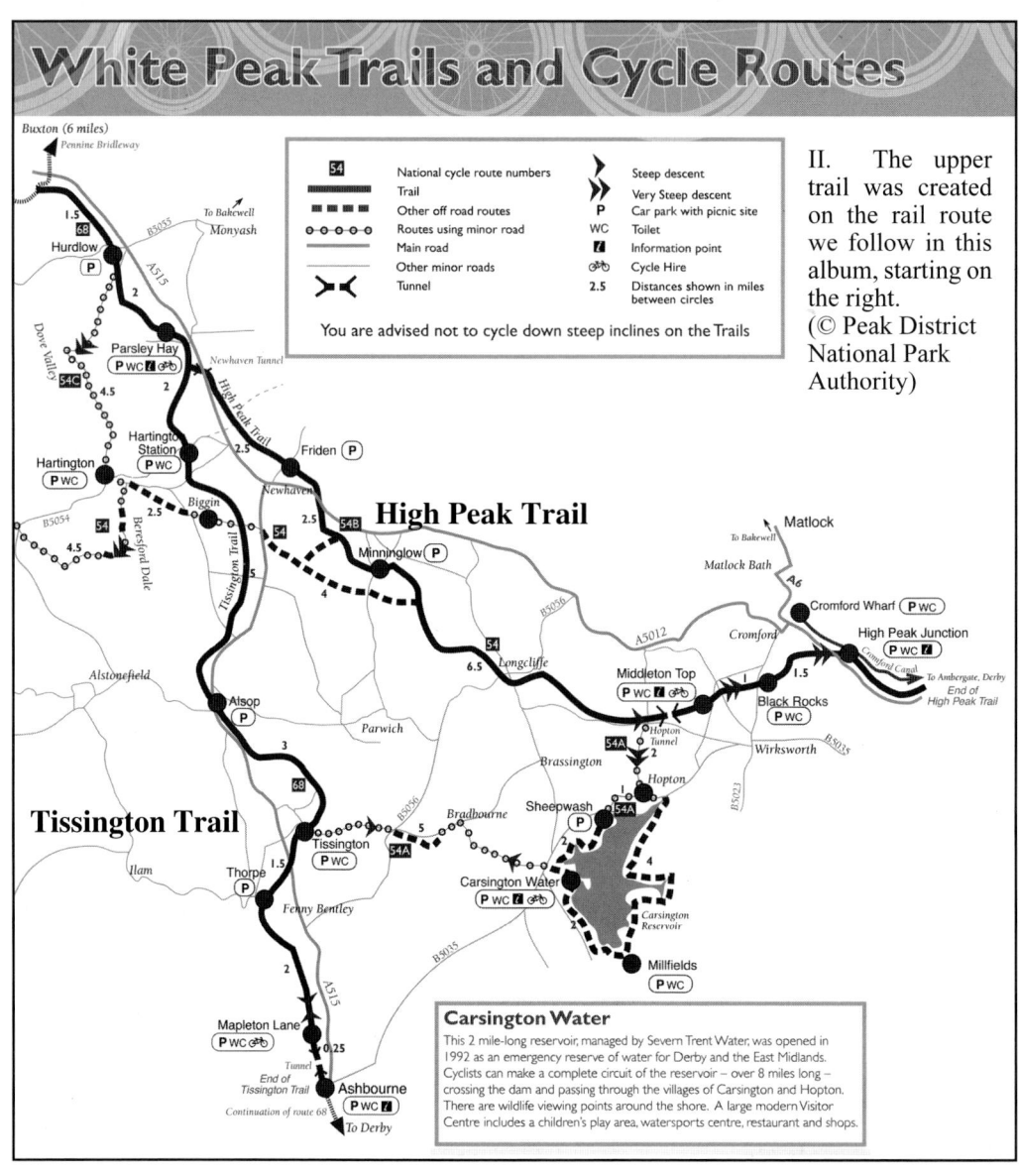

II. The upper trail was created on the rail route we follow in this album, starting on the right.
(© Peak District National Park Authority)

HISTORICAL BACKGROUND

The gap in the canal systems was the reason for planning a railway connection between the two so early. It was freight, not passengers, that was top priority.

Passed in 1825 was the Act for the Cromford & High Peak Railway. It was opened from Cromford Wharf to Hurdlow on 29th May 1830 and from Hurdlow to Whaley Bridge on 7th July 1831. Connection was made with the Manchester, Buxton, Matlock & Midlands Junction Railway at High Peak Junction, about ¾ of a mile from Cromford Wharf; this was brought into use on 21st February 1853. At the opposite end, an extension of ¼ of a mile linked it with the Stockport, Disley & Whaley Bridge Railway, which was opened on 17th August 1857.

Passengers were carried from 1855, but only in a braked van. They were supposed to walk up and down the inclines. Passenger service was abandoned in 1877, after a fatality. The London & North Western Railway leased the Cromford & High Peak Railway in 1861 and took it over fully in 1878. Horse traction ended in 1871, apart from on the Whaley Bridge incline. The Ladmanlow to Whaley Bridge section, at the north end of the route, closed in June 1892.

The LNWR became a major part of the London Midland & Scottish Railway upon the grouping of 1923. This formed most of the London Midland Region of British Railways with nationalisation in 1948.

The Middleton incline closed on 12th August 1963. The Friden-Parsley Hay section followed on 21st April 1967. In 1968, Derbyshire County Council and the Peak District National Park purchased the trackbed between Cromford Wharf and Hurdlow, for all to enjoy.

PASSENGER SERVICES

As stated, these were never provided specifically and people were only moved in one van in 1855-77. Thus only one of the three timetables shown here is relevant. Bradshaw did not justify including any. In 1861 only 161 passengers were carried.

A large number of route tours took place in the 1950s and 1960s, dedicated to railway admirers. The last day was amazing, as three trips were run. It was on 30th April 1967 and one pair of locos worked them. Your scribe (V.M.) was one of the visitors squeezed into a brake van. Many such views follow.

The service between Parsley Hay and Hindlow is detailed in our *Uttoxeter to Buxton* album, which also includes Ashbourne.

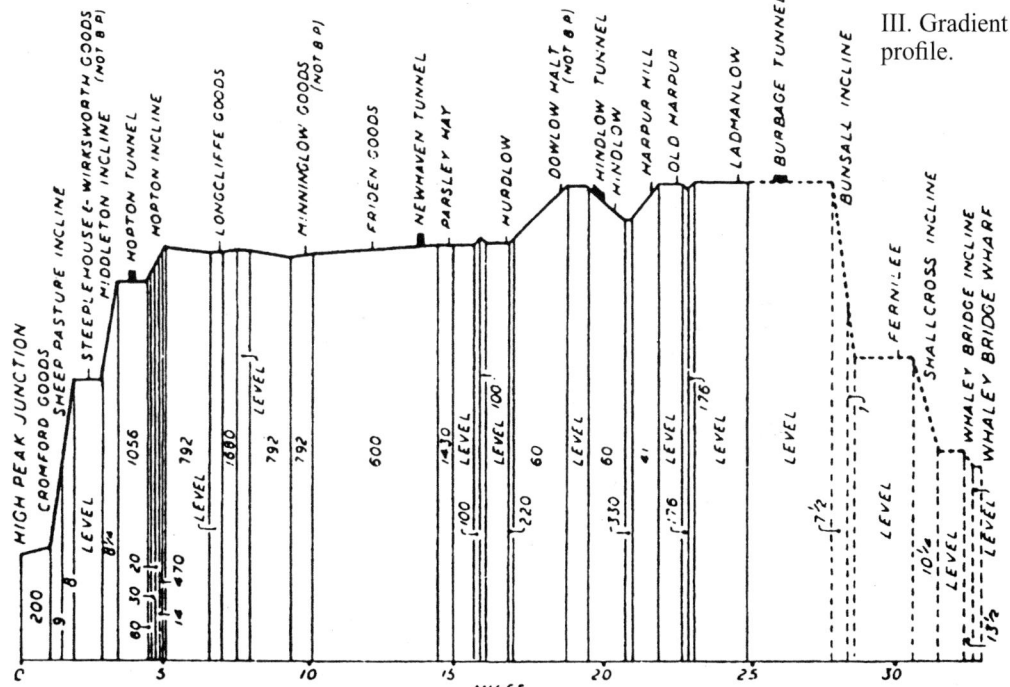

III. Gradient profile.

Particulars of Gradients.

Miles From	Miles To	Rising or Falling.	Gradient.	Between what Stations. From	Between what Stations. To	Locomotive or Stationary Engine.
0	1¼	Rising	1 in 120	High Peak Junction ...	Bottom of Sheep Pasture	Locomotive.
1¼	1¾	Rising	1 in 8½	Sheep-pasture Incline	......	Stationary.
1¾	3¼	Level	...	Steeplehouse	Middle Peak Yard ...	Locomotive.
3¼	3¾	Rising	1 in 8¼	Middleton Incline ...	... ...	Stationary.
3¾	5¼	Falling	1 in 1056	Middleton	Hopton	⎫
5¼	5½	Rising	1 in 14	Hopton Incline	......	⎪
5½	7	Falling	1 in 792	Hopton	Longcliffe	⎪
7	8¾	Level	...	Longcliffe	Minninglow	⎪
8¾	9¼	Falling	1 in 792	Longcliffe	Minninglow and Friden	⎬ Locomotive.
9¼	10¾	Rising	1 in 792	Minninglow	Friden	⎪
10¾	15	Rising	1 in 757	Minninglow	Parsley Hay	⎪
15	17½	Level	...	Parsley Hay	Hurdlow	⎪
17½	19½	Rising	1 in 60	Hurdlow	......	⎭
19½	29	Level	...	Hurdlow	Bunsall	
29	29¼	Falling	1 in 792	Hurdlow	Bunsall	
29¼	30¾	Falling	1 in 7¼	Bunsall Incline	......	Stationary.
30¾	33	Level	...	Bunsall	Shallcross	Locomotive.
33	33¼	Falling	1 in 10½	Shallcross Incline ...	......	Stationary.
33¼	33½	Level	...	Shallcross Yard	......	...
33½	33¾	Falling	1 in 18½	Whaley Bridge	......	Windlass.

Manchester,
April, 1891.

G. E. MAWBY,
District Superintendent.

Gradient details from the working timetable for April 1891.

Passenger timetable for 1874.

TIME TABLE.—Commencing April 1, 1891.

EXPLANATIONS OF REFERENCES.

C—Conditional Train. Runs when required only. | X—Stops when required for traffic purposes.
M—Mondays excepted. | S—Saturdays excepted.

Distance.	Week Days—Down Trains.	1	2	3	4	C 5	6	7	8	9
		a.m.		a.m.		p.m.				
...	High Peak Junction ... dep.	...	...	...	...	1 40	...	...	...	...
1	Cromford (Bottom of)	6 20	...	11 30	...	2 0	...	...	...	...
1¼	Sheep Pasture (Top of)	6 29	...	11 39	...	2 15	...	...	...	...
2¾	Steeplehouse	6 45	...	11 55	...	2 20	...	...	...	...
3	Middle Peak Yard	6 50	...	12 5	...	2 30	...	...	...	...
3½	Middleton (Top of)	7 0	...	12 20	...	2 40	...	...	...	...
5	Hopton (Top of)	7 30	...	12 50	...	3 0	...	...	...	...
6½	Manystones Siding	X	...	X	...	...	...	...	...	...
7	Longcliffe	7 53	...	1 30	...	3 8	...	...	...	...
9	Bloore's Siding	X	...	X	...	...	...	...	...	...
10	Minninglow Sidings	X	...	X	...	...	...	...	...	...
12½	Friden	8 19	...	2 10	...	3 28	...	...	...	...
15	Parsley Hay	8 39	...	2 30	...	3 38	...	...	...	...
17	Hurdlow (Bottom of)	8 47	...	2 50	...	3 45	...	...	...	...
19	Hurdlow (Top of) ... arr.	9 2	...	3 5	...	3 50	...	...	...	...
19	Hurdlow (Top of) ... dep.	9 7	...	8 15	...	...	...	...	...	...
19⅓	Briggs' Siding	X	...	X	...	...	...	...	...	...
21	Hindlow	9 15	...	8 30	...	4 0	...	...	...	...
23¾	Harpur Hill	9 30	...	3 43	...	4 10	...	...	...	...
26¼	Ladmanlow	9 47	...	4 35	...	4 20	...	...	...	...
29¼	Bunsall (Top of)	10 0	...	4 45	...	4 30	...	...	...	...
32¼	Shallcross (Bottom of)	10 45	...	5 30	...	5 0	...	...	...	...
33½	Whaley Bridge ... arr.	11 5	...	...	...	5 10	...	...	...	...

Working timetable for April 1891.

Working timetable for September 1956.

WEEKDAYS — PARSLEY HAY AND MIDDLETON

DOWN

Mileage M	Mileage C																
					J	J	J	J	J		J			J			
						8.10 am Empties from Buxton	7.55 am Empties from Buxton				1.35 pm from Hopton Quarry						
					74			74	75		74			75			
						FX	FO										
					am	am	am	PM	am		PM			PM			
0	0	PARSLEY HAY	arr	..		8 53	8 55	..	..	..	..	..	..	..	..	..	..
			dep			9 25	9 25										
2	26	Friden	arr	..	← Bank	9 40	9 40		..	..	..	..	..	..	..	..	..
			dep						11 55								
7	63	Longcliffe	arr	..		..	..	← Intake Sidings	12 25	..	..	..	..	..	..	..	..
			dep						1 10								
10	16	Hopton (Top)	arr	..	..	..	..		1 23	..	1 45	..	..	..	..	..	..
			dep		8• 15			12• 0	2 0		1 50			2 40			
11	8	Hopton Quarry	arr	..	8 20	..	..	..	..	..	..	..	..	..	..	..	..
			dep		8 30												
11	31	MIDDLETON (TOP)	arr	..	8 40	..	..	12 5	2 5	..	1 58	..	..	2 45	..	..	..

UP

Mileage M	Mileage C																
					J	J		J	J	J		J	J	J			
									To Hindlow			To Middleton	To Hindlow				
					74	75		74		74		74		75			
									SO				SX				
					am	am		am	PM	PM		PM	PM	PM			
0	0	MIDDLETON (TOP)	dep	..	7 35	9 5	..	11 15	..	12 30	..	..	..	2 30	..	..	..
0	23	Hopton Quarry	arr		7 45					12 40							
			dep	..	8 5	..	..	..	..	..	..	1 35	..	..	..	..	..
1	15	Hopton (Top)	arr		8• 10	9 15		11• 20				1 45		2 35			
			dep	..	..	9 35	..	..	..	..	..	1 50	..	..	..	..	..
1	77	Harboro' Sdgs	arr			9 40											
			dep	..		9 55	..		..	..	..	..	..	..	..	..	..
3	48	Longcliffe	arr		← Bank	10 5		← Intake Sidings									
			dep	..		11 5	..		..	..	..	..	..	..	..	..	..
9	5	Friden	arr			11 35											
			dep	..		..	..		12 30	..	..	..	1 55	..	..	..	..
11	31	PARSLEY HAY	arr						12 45				2 13				

HIGH PEAK JUNCTION

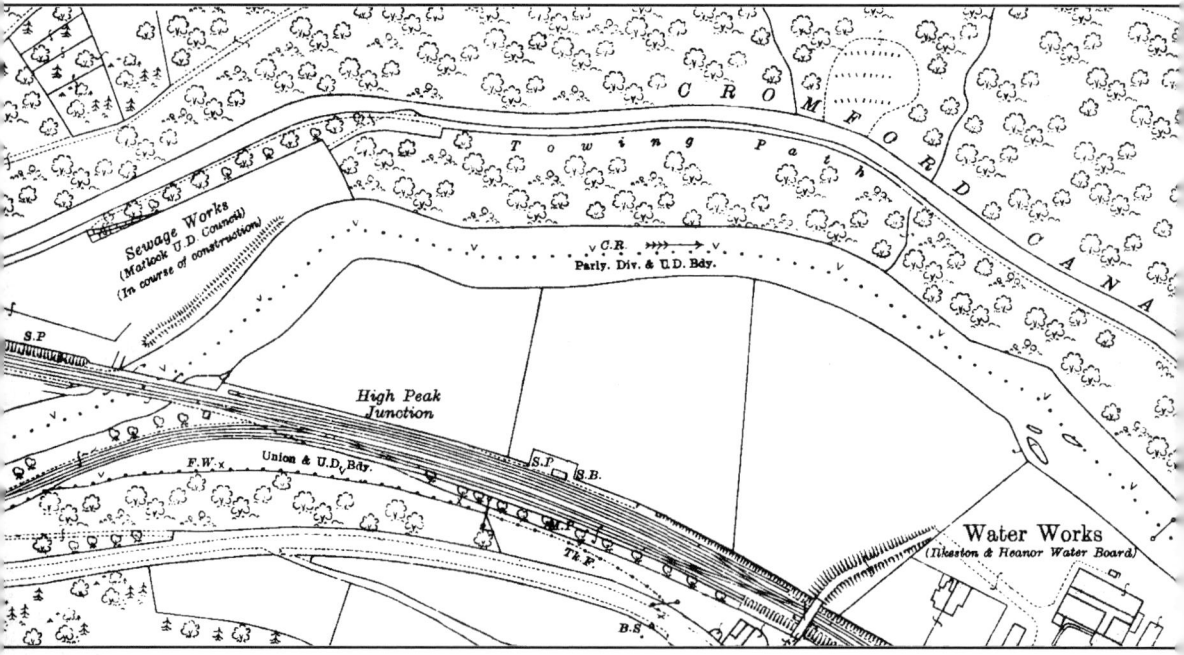

IV. This 1922 map has the River Derwent curving across its centre part and the double track of the Ambergate to Buxton line on the bridge across it. Curving on the left is the C&HPR and the canal is across the upper part.

1. The west end of the exchange sidings is seen in 1931. The roof of the signal box is in the distance. (R.Humm coll.)

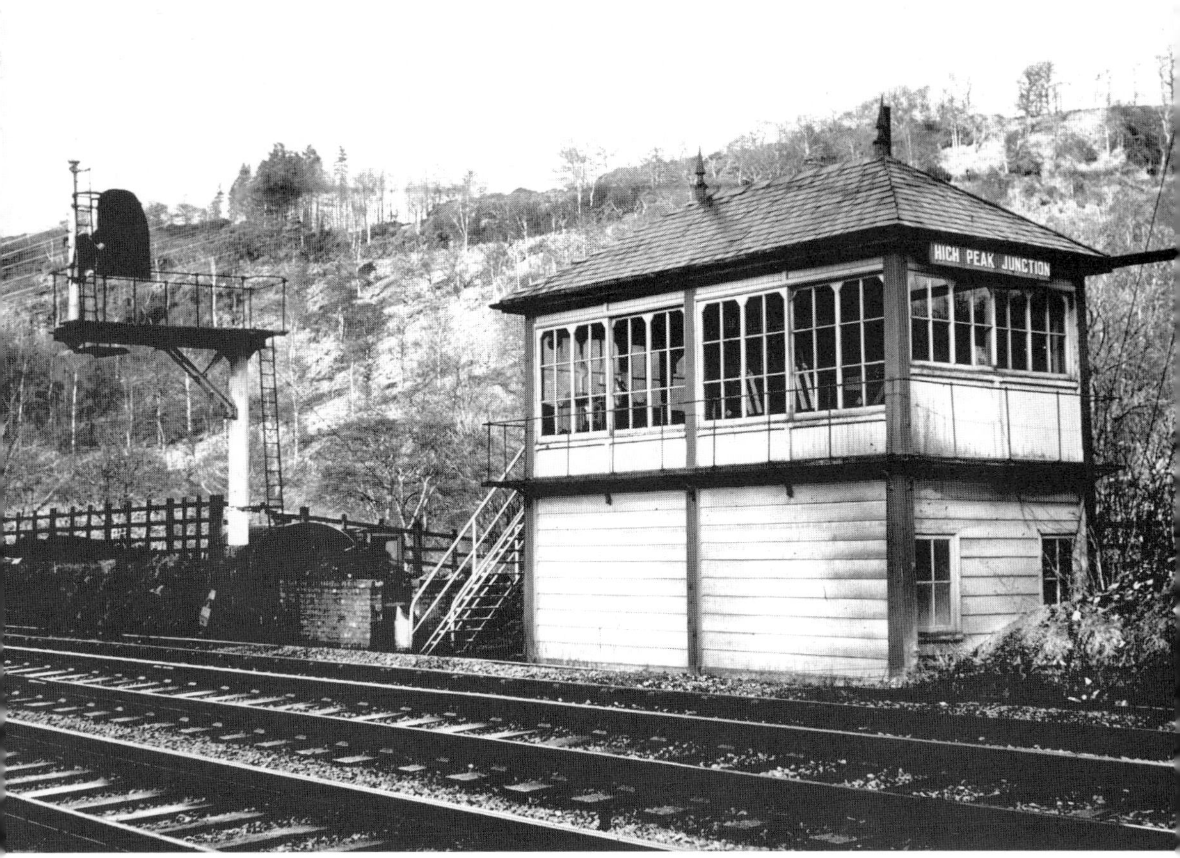

2. The box had 20 levers and was worked from 18th June 1901 to 29th October 1967. Much limestone is evident. (A.F.Bullimore)

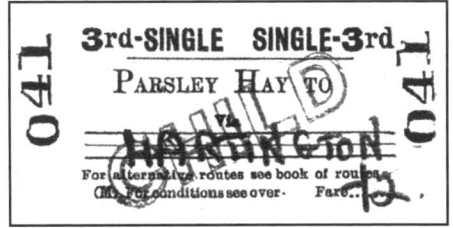

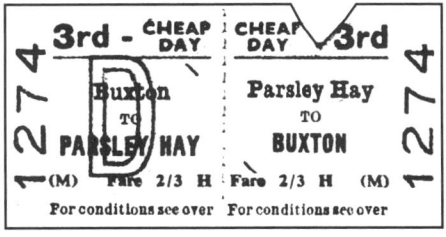

CROMFORD WHARF

3. We move west and find part of the wharf, with LMS 2F 0-6-0 no. 27505 in attendance. ANTHRACITE refers to an expensive, hard form of coal from South Wales, almost smokeless and with a high calorific value. (R.Humm coll.)

4. It is 1949 and this 2F had received its BR number of 58862 recently. It has the good fortune of a spare coupling. (R.Humm coll.)

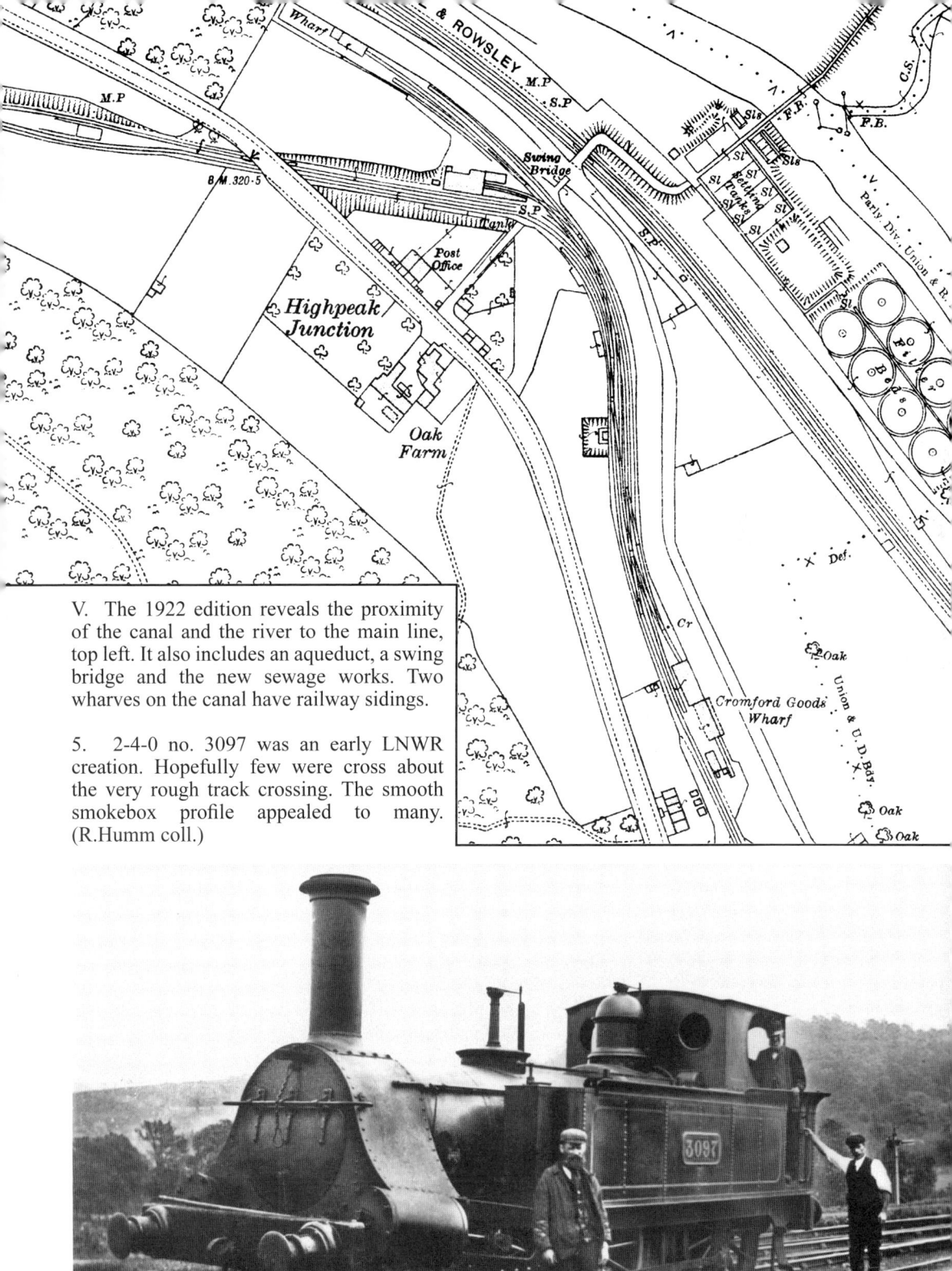

V. The 1922 edition reveals the proximity of the canal and the river to the main line, top left. It also includes an aqueduct, a swing bridge and the new sewage works. Two wharves on the canal have railway sidings.

5. 2-4-0 no. 3097 was an early LNWR creation. Hopefully few were cross about the very rough track crossing. The smooth smokebox profile appealed to many. (R.Humm coll.)

6. Old LNWR tenders are gathered here in 1931 to serve as adjustable balance water tanks on the incline when in need of balancing. The Cromford Incline was 580yds long, with a gradient of 1 in 9. Spring water was available here to fill these tanks. It was also used by the line's locomotives. (R.Humm coll.)

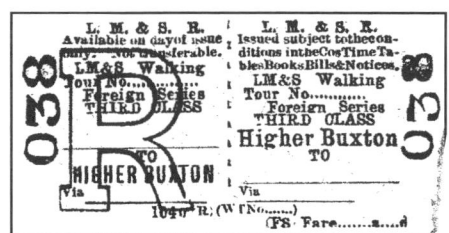

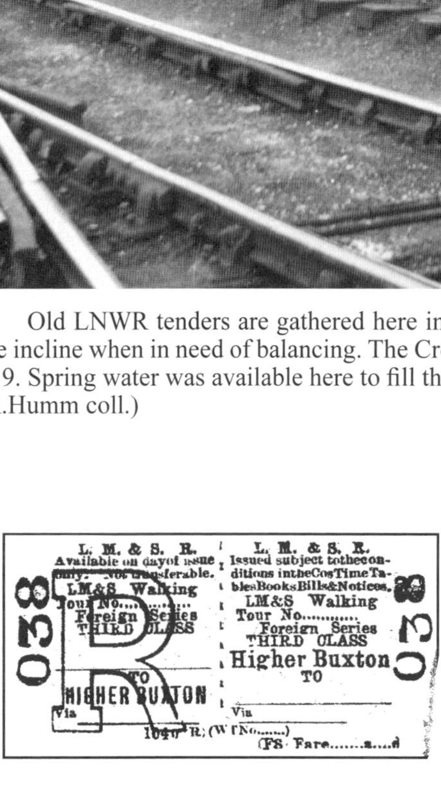

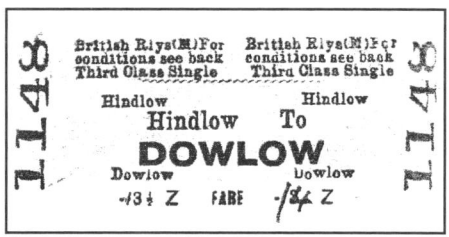

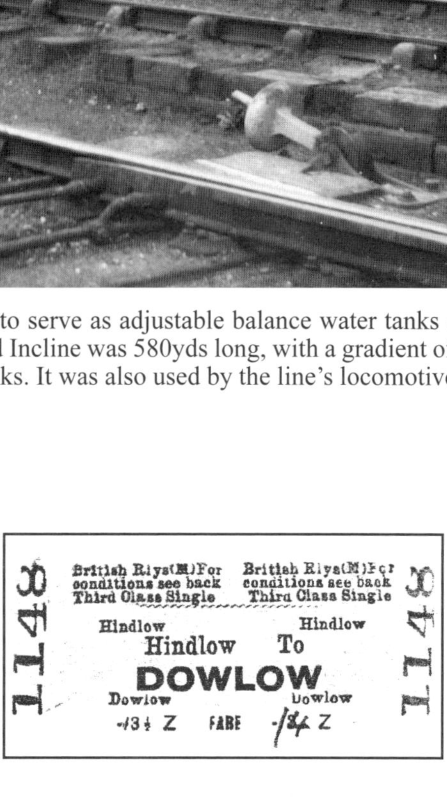

7. Centre in this 1931 photograph is a rectangular sheet running-in signal on top of a pole. The snow was always a problem for delivery horses on the surfaced roads. These were still being extended at this time. The location is near the bottom of the map. (R.Humm coll.)

8. Ex-North London Railway class 2F no. 58850 had been retired to the country. It is seen on 15th June 1951 displaying its early square glazing. This was the terminus of the C&HPR until 1853. (T.G.Wassell/Photos from the Fifties)

9. Sadly, no details were recorded, except the date. This was 25th April 1953; the snow was deemed late, but not so at 320ft above sea level. The swing bridge served the road on the right. Often limestone dust looked like remains of snow. (R.Humm coll.)

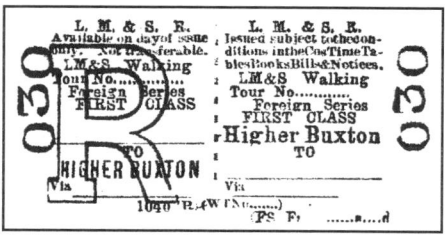

10. This was the engine shed and it was at the north end of the track layout. It appears to have had a side door to allow coal in from canal barges, in the early days. Coal consumed here in 1963 amounted to 151 tons and wood to four wagonloads. The shed was later demolished. (J.Suter coll.)

11. The transit shed offered good access to all forms of transport. On the right is a canopy to protect road vehicles' rear ends. The curved white arch is part of a railway loading gauge. (P.G.Barnes)

12. At the other end of the shed was this extensive protected loading area. Both photographs were taken on 22nd August 1994. The first rails were in 4ft lengths and were cast by the Butterley Company in Ripley and fitted on raised stone blocks, not wooden sleepers. (P.G.Barnes)

13. Our final pair of views of this location reveals the area that would have been used by passengers in the mid-19th Century. This record is from July 1955 and includes a balance tank wagon, which would contain water, when necessary. (J.Suter coll.)

14. This similar panorama is from 16th August 2008 and shows the original buildings used again as the High Peak Junction Workshops. The High Peak Trail now ends east of here. Two brake vans rest in retirement on the left. (P.G.Barnes)

15. This 1964 record is unusual for revealing buffer defects. Big crosses and small words were rarely seen in the system, it seems. Haulage on the inclines was by means of a rope formed of a number of steel wires. (A.F.Bullimore)

16. In this uphill view from Cromford Wharf we can witness the means by which the straight cable was controlled on curves such as these. (Colour-Rail.com)

SHEEP PASTURE

17. We witness the chaining of a balance tank (an ex-LNWR tender) to the rope at the bottom of the incline in 1897. Much of the water was consumed by locomotives and some was used for domestic purposes. (R.Humm coll.)

18. A 1949 panorama from the bridge includes an amazing number of tanks to create a suitable balance weight on the incline. Instructions were listed for the enginemen, firemen, hangers-on and planemen. The latter were at the bottom of the incline and issued signals to the crew. (R.Humm coll.)

19. A party of visitors is allowed to witness assembly work on 25th April 1953. Many wagons with plain boards had been repaired cheaply after World War II bombing. (R.Humm coll.)

20. The reason for the timber on the sleepers in the previous picture now becomes apparent. The main cable pulleys are also clearer here. The incline was 711yds long at a 1 in 8 gradient. (D.Lawrence/Photos from the Fifties)

21. A view in the other direction shows the ground frame cabin from where the two points were controlled. They controlled the two very short lines to the catch pit, which is central. (R.Humm coll.)

22. This downhill view is from 1931 and here is a fine presentation of cable supports. Near the bottom of the incline, the two running tracks widen out and pass on each side of a large sleeper-lined pit, into which lead two spurs from catch points situated above the pit. They are seen in the previous picture. (R.Humm coll.)

Sheep Pasture Incline Top

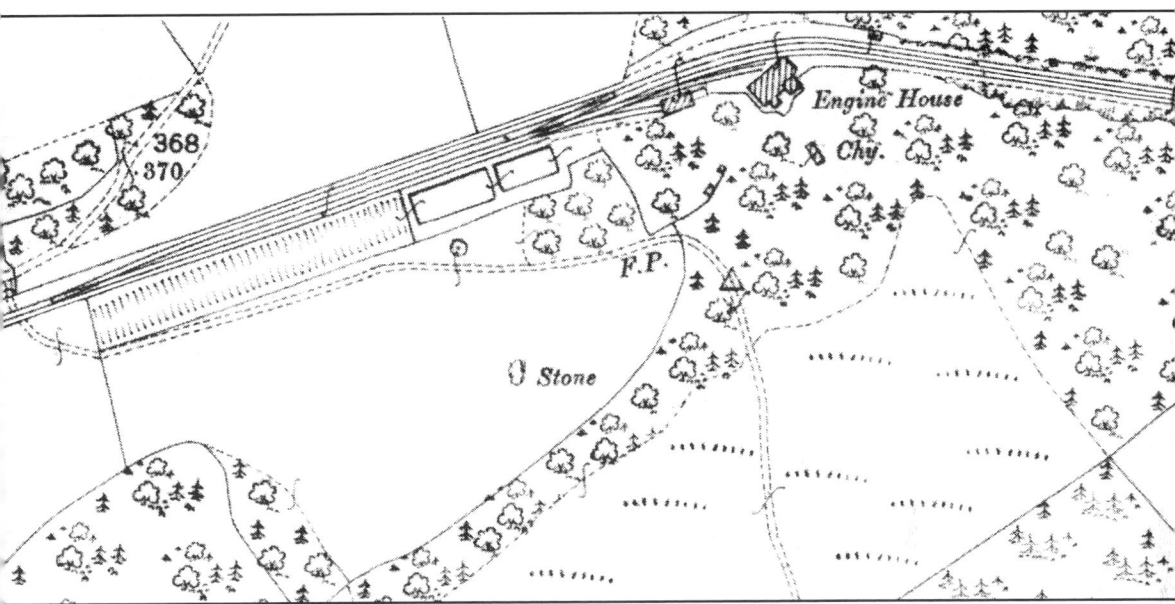

VI. The 1922 survey shows a layout which appears never to have changed. The engine shed was blown down in a massive storm in 1963, but was not rebuilt.

23. On the rise near the top of the incline are three wagons, which must be braked. The winding engine was a relatively modern twin-cylinder horizontal type, which drove the original flywheel and pulley through bevel gears. It was built in 1883, and its cylinders of 17ins bore by 24ins stroke were supplied with steam at 80 PSI from an old locomotive boiler, which was fired mainly with wood. (Colour-Rail.com)

24. We have sight of the summit in this record from October 1931. Trees were scarce at this height. The white knob on the right is a weight on a point lever, which acted as an automatic return. (R.Humm coll.)

25. The water tanks appear again as LMS 0-4-0ST no. 7000 waits on 12th October 1940. It was listed as 0F and was built by Kitsons, along with four others. 401 runs were made on the incline in March 1961. (H.C.Casserley)

26. It is 10th July 1959 and we can examine the local engine shed, along with the body of a brake van, which seems to be used as a workshop. (R.Humm coll.)

27. We cross one of the shed's reservoirs and find no. 47000, which we met as no. 7000 in picture 25. The extra number came from BR formation in 1948. Loaded wagons handled in March 1961 numbered 630 and empties 473. (R.Humm coll.)

28. Here is the peak of the Peak climb and on the left is the Winding Engine House, which had been abbreviated on map VI. Electric power was provided here in the final years of winding. (R.Humm coll.)

29. The other aspect of the Engine House was recorded on 20th July 2000, along with the Peak Trail and the all-important plaque. (M.P.Turvey)

STEEPLEHOUSE

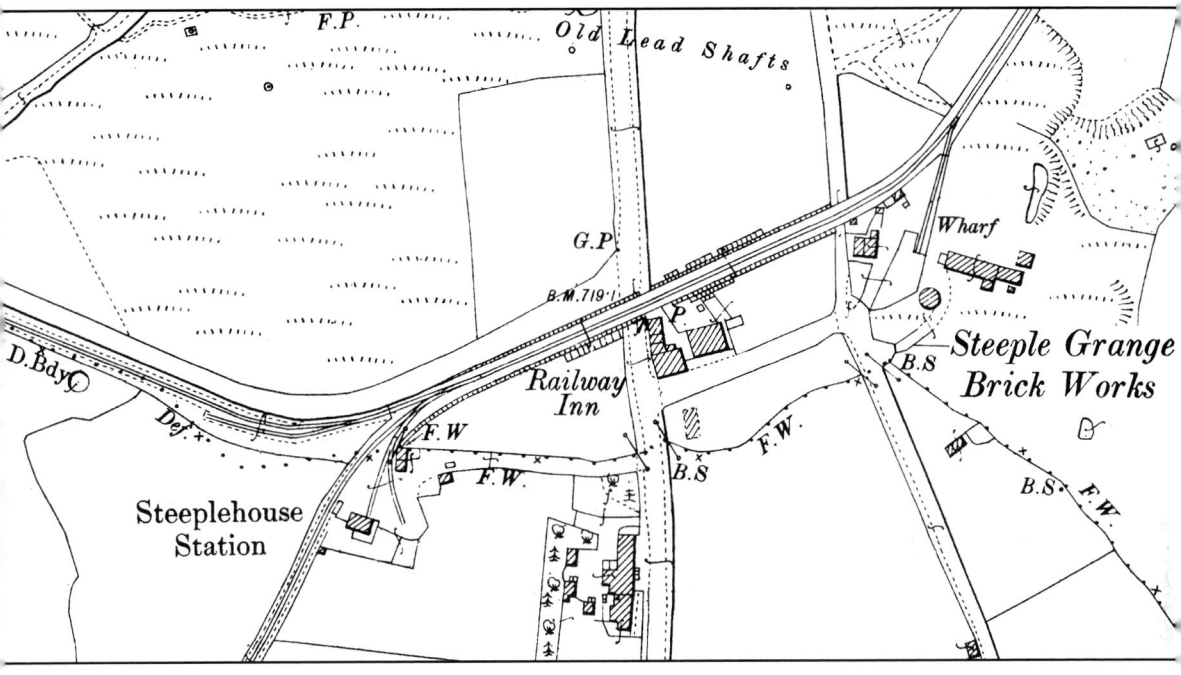

VII. The 1898 edition has the route of our journey from top right to the lower left. The line to the lower border ran towards Wirksworth.

30. The map shows this gate; it was over a ½ mile long private siding. It was the start of the Killer Branch, now the Steeple Grange Light Railway; see pictures 108, onwards. The goods yard tracks are close to the cottage. (J.Alsop coll.)

WEST OF STEEPLEHOUSE

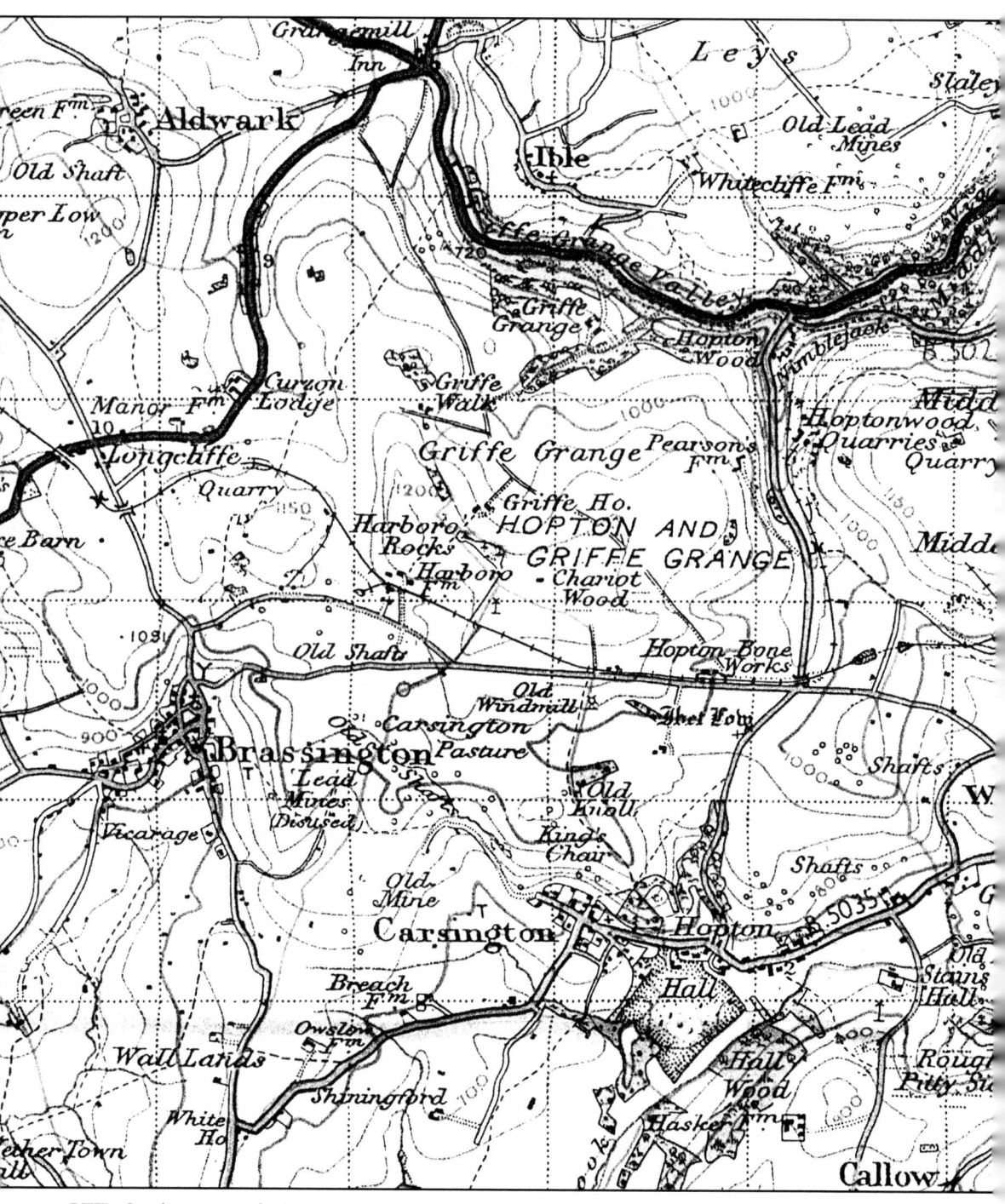

VIII. Our journey so far is on the right page of this map from 1947, which is scaled at 2ins to 1 mile. Highpeak Junction is shown west of the tunnel on the right, whereas it was to the east. Moreover, the mineral track is marked curving between the A6 and the river before joining the main line from Ambergate to Buxton. The C&HP line is annotated in full, but the connection with the branch line to Wirksworth is not clear. It is contained within our album of that title, as is the Steeple Grange

Light Railway. This began operation in 1986 on part of a trackbed, shown below the B5036 and the words 'Old Shafts'. It also appears from picture 108 onwards in this volume. On the left page are connections to two quarries and one factory. Middleton itself spans the join of the two pages, as does much of the incline. Hopton Tunnel is just on the left page.

31. A connection ran south to link with the Midland Railway for goods and mineral traffic, in the early days. The connection to Wirksworth is within this view from 26th March 1932. (R.Humm coll.)

MIDDLETON

32. This much rebuilt early diesel locomotive is seen at Derbyshire Stone at Middleton on 25th July 1964. It is believed to have originated as a petrol locomotive built by the Kent Construction Company of Ashford, Kent, in about 1925. It survives in private hands in Shropshire. (A.R.Etherington/A.Neale coll.)

33. Also photographed at Middleton on 25th July 1964 was this early Motor Rail diesel locomotive. Curtains hang halfway across the wagons to minimise dust during their loading. Curtains are on the loco also. (A.R.Etherington/A.Neale coll.)

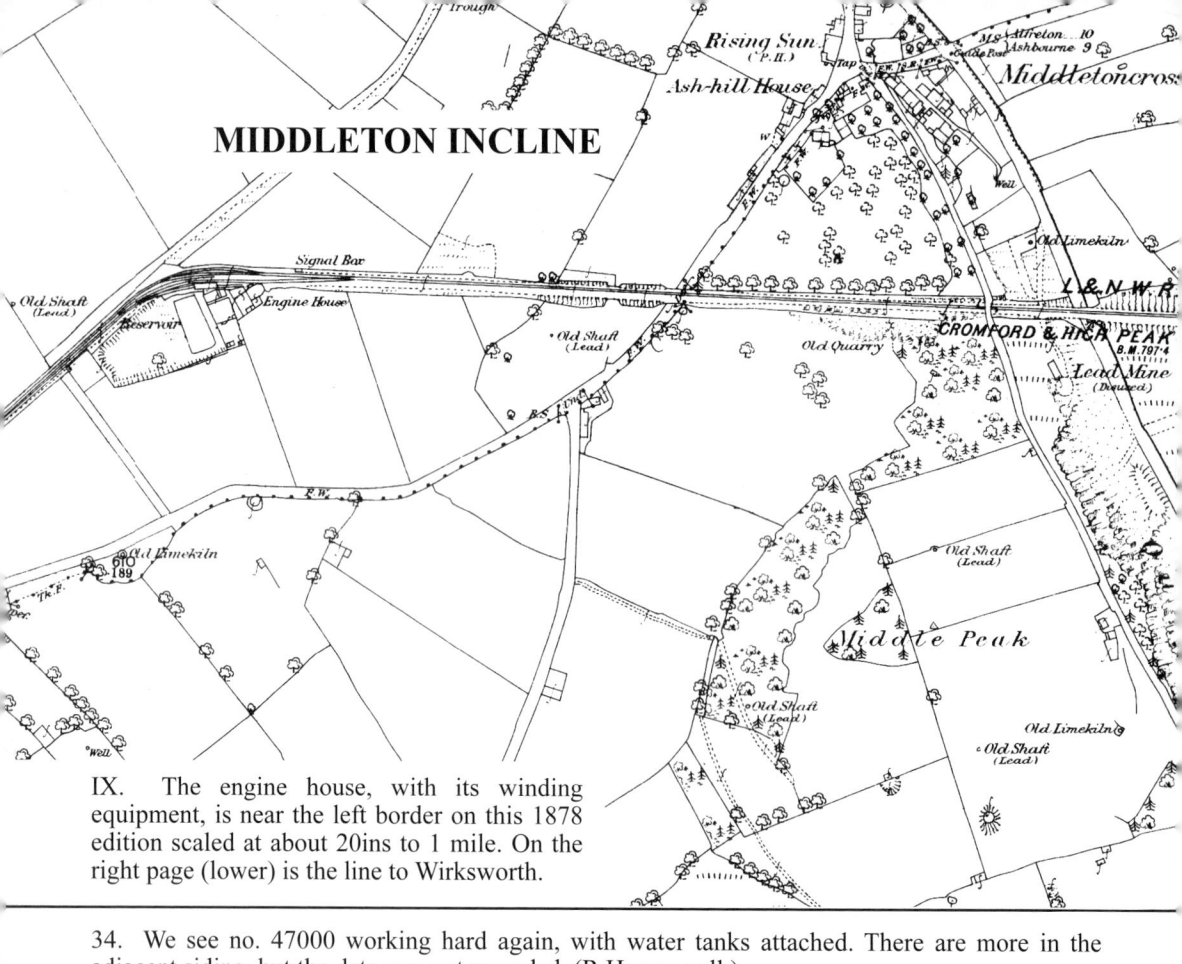

MIDDLETON INCLINE

IX. The engine house, with its winding equipment, is near the left border on this 1878 edition scaled at about 20ins to 1 mile. On the right page (lower) is the line to Wirksworth.

34. We see no. 47000 working hard again, with water tanks attached. There are more in the adjacent siding, but the date was not recorded. (R.Humm coll.)

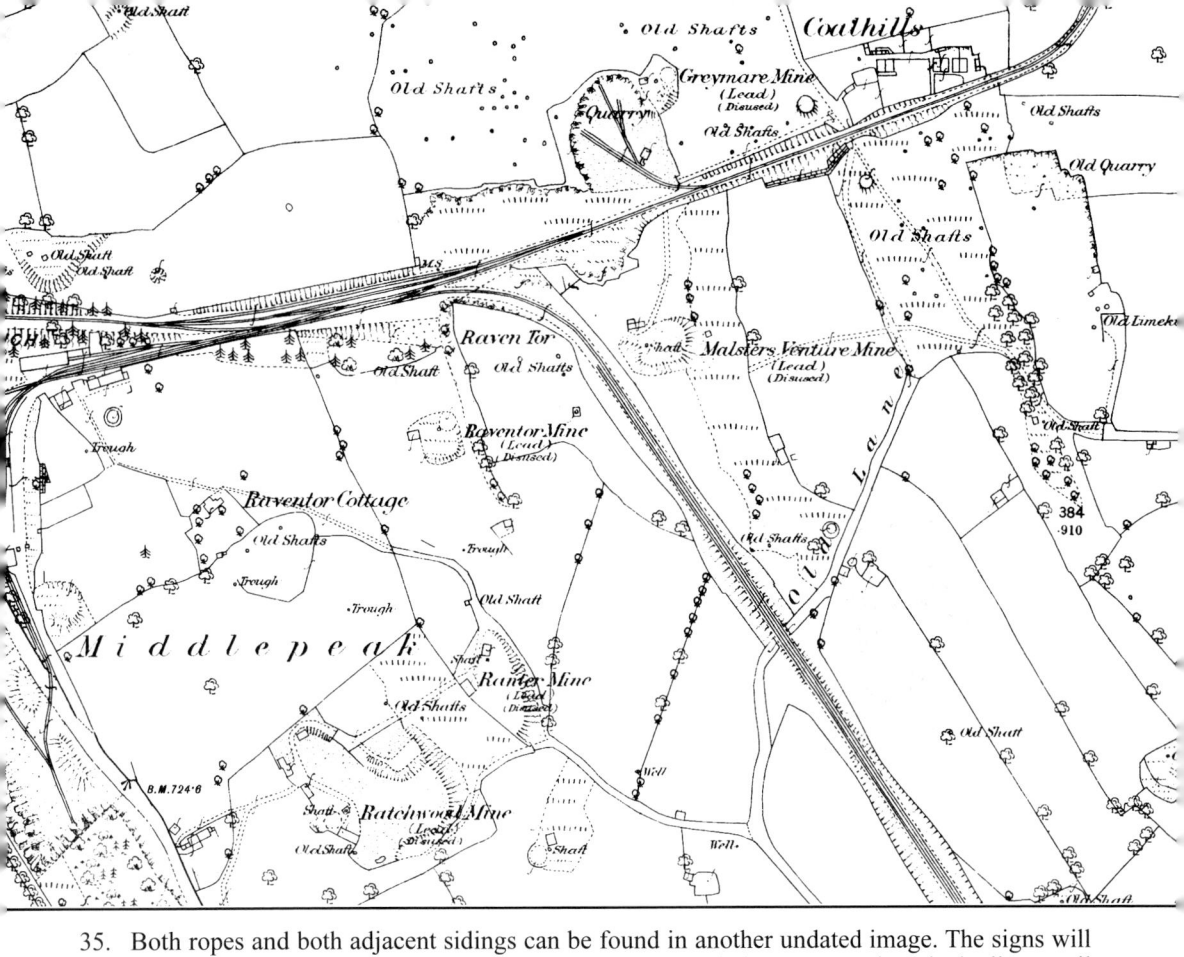

35. Both ropes and both adjacent sidings can be found in another undated image. The signs will carry the words seen on boards at the foot of other inclines. Chains were used on the inclines until 1856, when hemp ropes came into use. Steel wire ropes were to be found from 1861, onwards. (D.Lawrence/Photos of the Fifties)

Middleton Top

36. We are looking outwards down the incline on 15th April 1961, with catch points and serious railway students evident. At Middleton Top, there is a visitor centre belonging to Derbyshire County Council and the Engine House belongs to the Derbyshire Archaeological Society. (J.Langford)

37. Looking at the same location, but in the other direction, we can study many interesting details, including the coupling position and that of the shunter. (R.Humm coll.)

38. Near the locomotive shed is class J94 0-6-0ST no. 68013. On the right is the main water tank and its filler bay. (D.Lawrence/Photos of the Fifties)

39. An SLS Railtour was recorded on 25th April 1953 and making a rare appearance are the steps which allow members in and out of the open wagons. They could also use the two brake vans. The other details are in caption 45. (R.Humm coll.)

40. No. 58857 was 2F 0-6-0T, a type introduced by the North London Railway in 1879 and inherited by the LMS, in 1923. (R.Humm coll.)

41. The engine house was the centre of many diverse engineering activities locally, as evident here. The incline was the longest running in the 20th Century at 708yds. The gradient was 1 in 8½. (R.Humm coll.)

42. Taking water in 1967 is no. 68012, a class J94 0-6-0ST. Following the end of World War II, a large number of these were bought from the Ministry of Supply. The earlier tank appears to have been replaced by a retired Lancashire boiler. (A.F.Bullimore)

43. The High Peak Trail is on the right in this panorama from 27th August 2016. The seat encourages many to dwell on happy memories or great astonishment. (P.G.Barnes)

HOPTON

44. A record from the 1930s includes limestone outcrops as is common. The tunnel was 457yds in length and was level. Hopton Incline was on a gradient of 1 in 14. (J.Alsop coll.)

45. The SLS tour of 25th April 1953 was hauled by nos 58860 and 58856, ex-NLR 0-6-0Ts. They are approaching Hopton Tunnel. The tour included Wirksworth and Buxton. (M.Dart coll.)

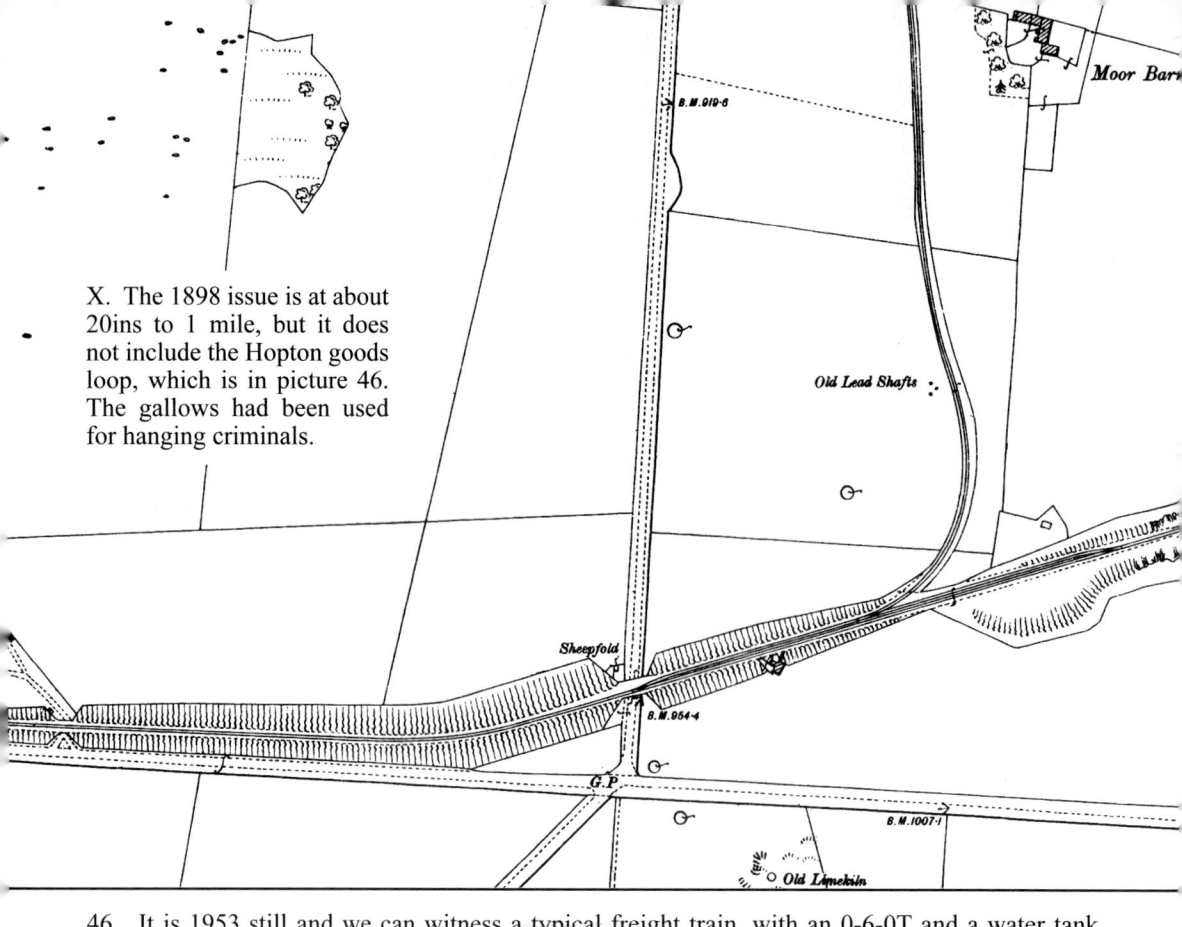

X. The 1898 issue is at about 20ins to 1 mile, but it does not include the Hopton goods loop, which is in picture 46. The gallows had been used for hanging criminals.

46. It is 1953 still and we can witness a typical freight train, with an 0-6-0T and a water tank leading. Behind the guards van is Hopton Goods loop. (R.Humm coll.)

Hopton Stone Branch

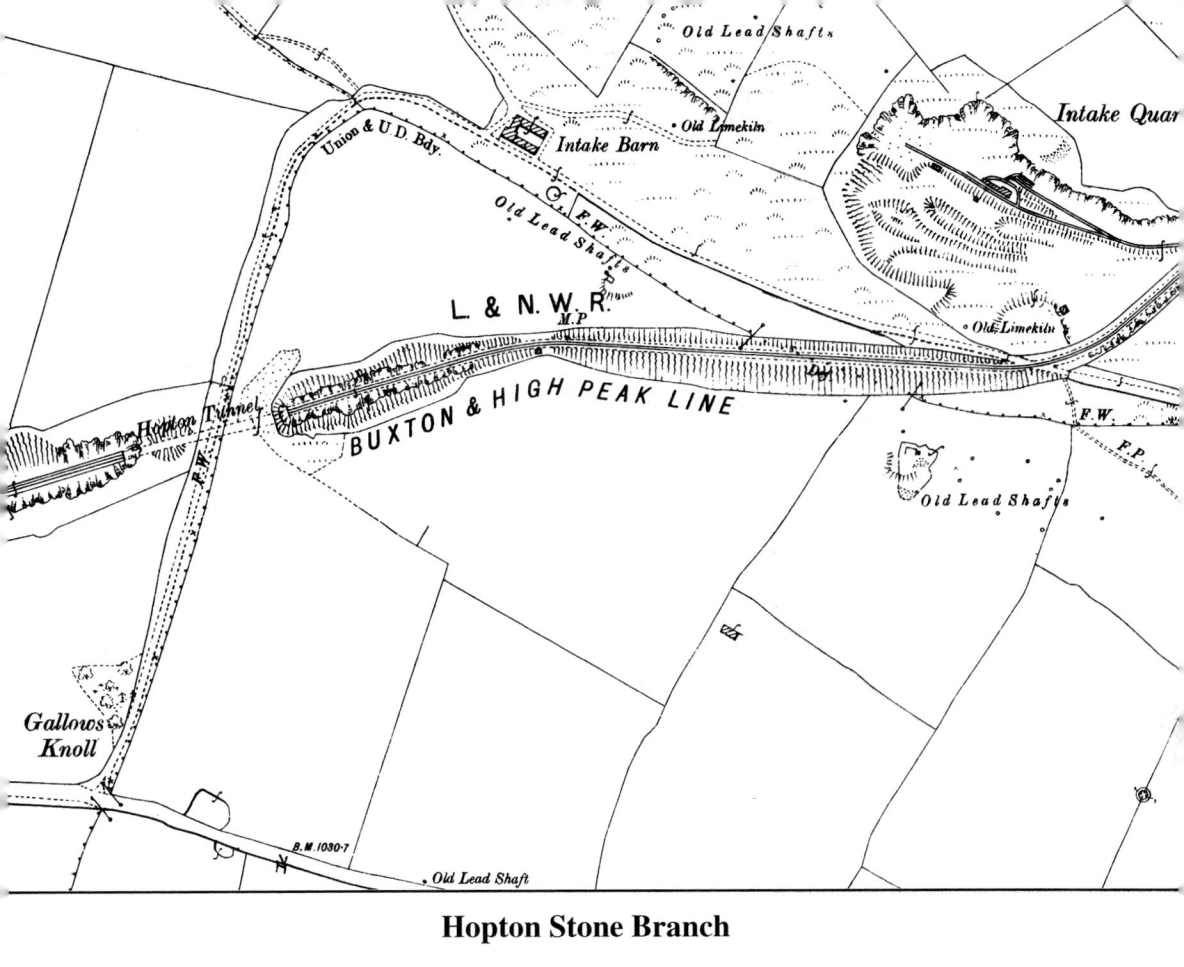

47. We witness a loaded train creeping off the branch some time in 1953. Tree growth since picture 44 is notable. (R.Humm coll.)

48. We now have two very different steam locomotives photographed at Hoptonwood Stone Firms Ltd on 17th September 1955. The upper picture shows a diminutive 'Yorktown' class Peckett 0-4-0ST (Peckett 1669 of 1924) built up from narrow gauge components and having only 7in cylinders. (B.Mettam/A. Neale coll.)

← 49. This shows their 1929 Sentinel 100 HP geared vertical boilered locomotive, Sentinel no. 7925. Massive conveyor belts adorn the skyline.
(B.Mettam/A.Neale coll.)

↓ XI. At the top is the Hopton Stone Branch, while this 1898 extract has a raw material producer on the left. Its output was bone manure, which contained rare minerals. Fluorite and baryte ores have also been processed here. The map is scaled at about 15ins to 1 mile.

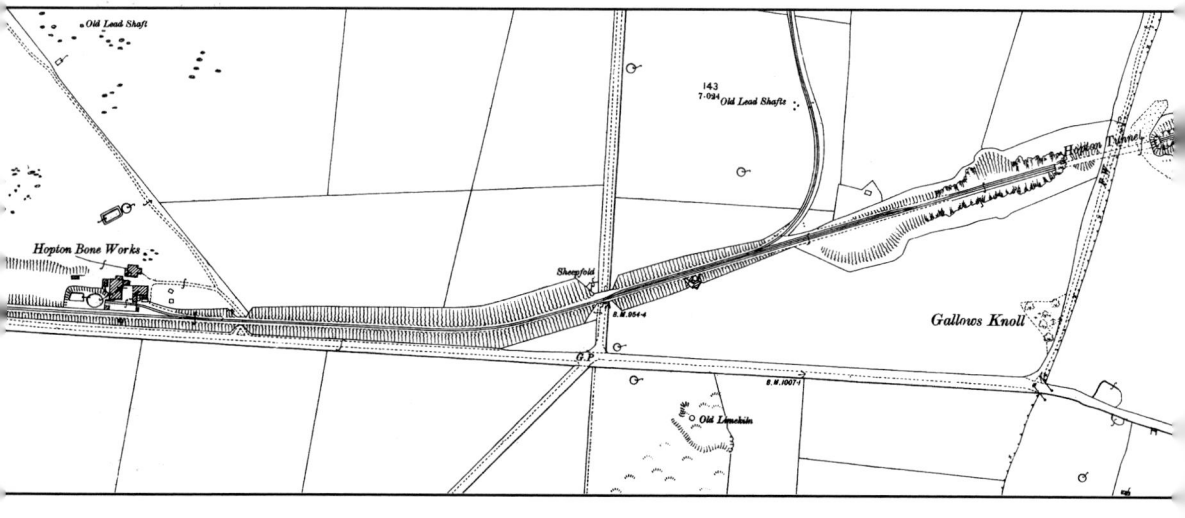

50. The massive Hopton bone processing factory is seen in the presence of class J94 0-6-0ST no. 68012, not long before route closure. The incline is on the left. (Colour-Rail.com)

XII. The brickworks siding is shown on the 1922 edition, which is scaled at about 20ins to 1 mile.

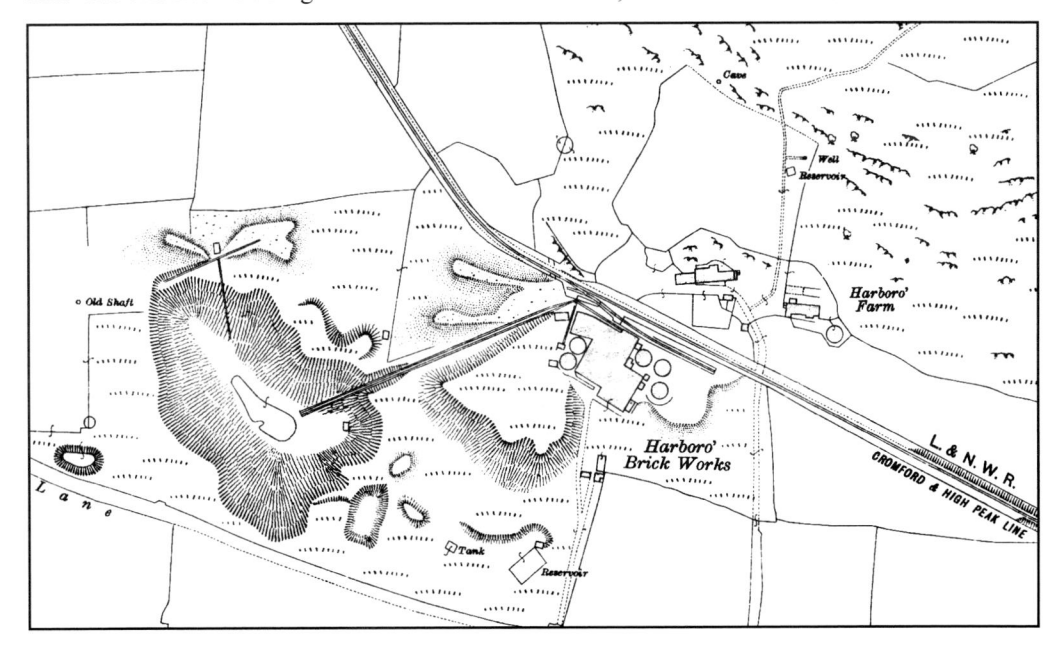

Hopton Incline

51. This impressive view at the top of the incline features 2-4-0T no. 3049, which had been rebuilt from a Crewe Goods. This was the steepest to have been worked by direct adhesion of a steam locomotive. It had been chain-hauled until 1877. (R.Humm coll.)

52. This accident took place on 6th October 1937. The train consisted of four wagons plus a brake van, and was thought to be running at about 45mph. It was the 8.35am Middleton Top to Parsley Hay, hauled by LMS class 2F 0-6-0T no. 27521. There were only 15 of this type left by 1945. (H.Townley/Bentley coll.)

53. This is the panorama found on the Hopton Incline from the leading brake van of the SLS North Staffordshire, Buxton and Cromford & High Peak Rail Tour. It was the 4.52pm from Parsley Hay on 15th April 1961. The engines were 0-6-0STs nos 68030 and 68013. (J.Langford)

54. The end is nigh. It is 1967 and working hard is an ex-MOS class J94 0-6-0ST. No. 68012 is losing steam from where it should not. (A.F.Bullimore)

55. From the top of Hopton Incline, we can enjoy the vista and examine an unaltered tender used for locomotive water. The short siding was for safety measures on the approach to the steep incline downwards. (Bentley coll.)

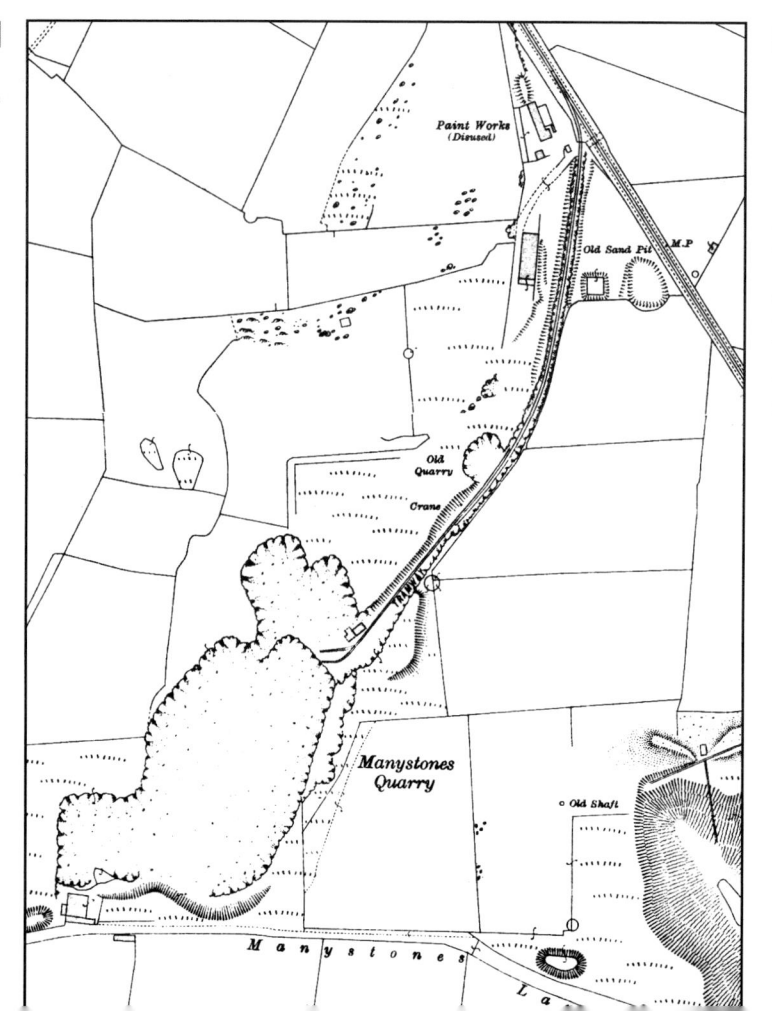

WEST OF HOPTON

XIII. The private quarry sidings shown lower centre on this 1922 map were owned by Hopton Wood Stone Ltd. The Old Shaft had been used for lead mining.

LONGCLIFFE GOODS

XIV. Longcliffe is lower right on this 1947 map at 1in to 1 mile. Our route runs to Parsley Hay, which is top left. From there northwards, double track is shown.

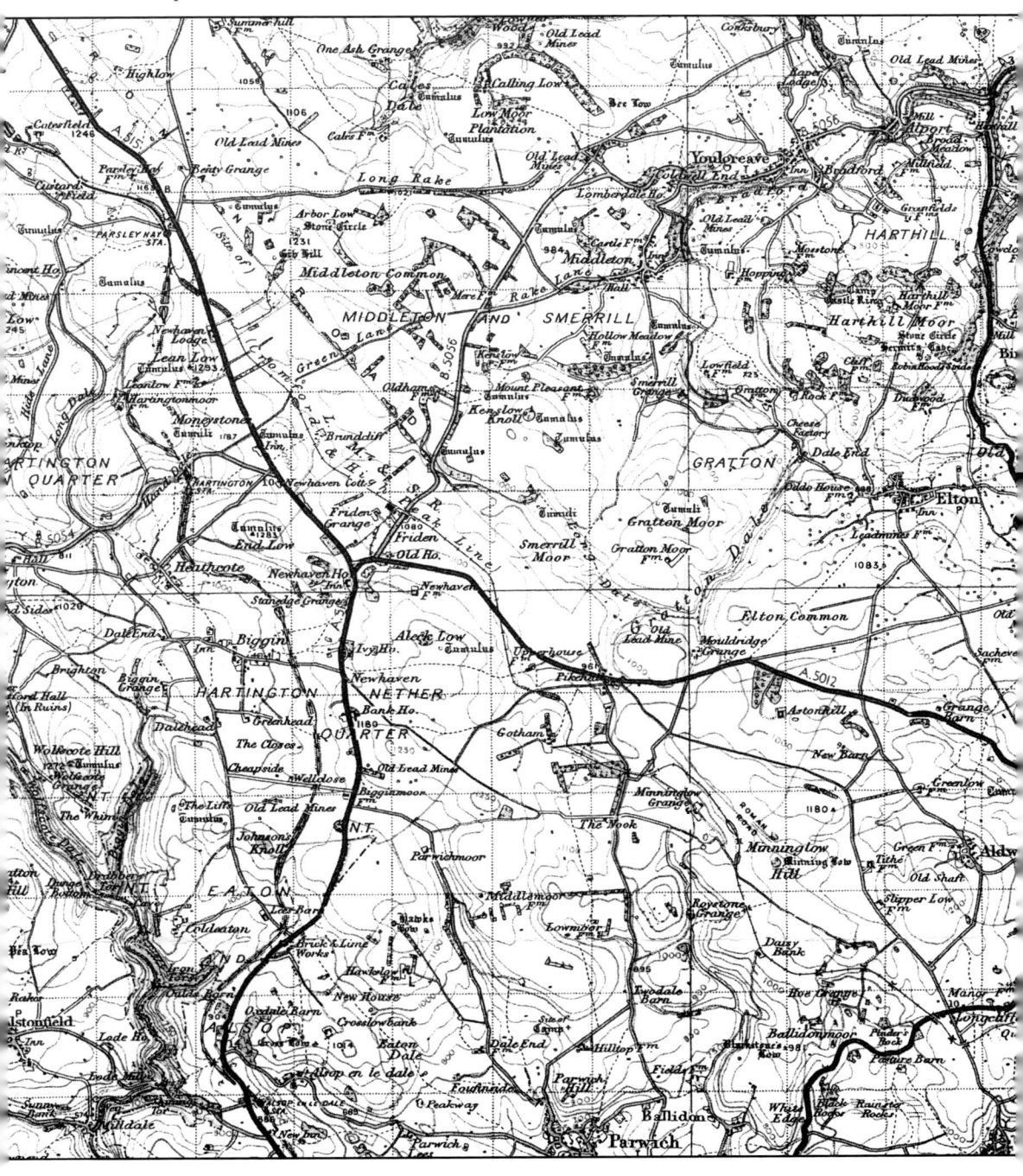

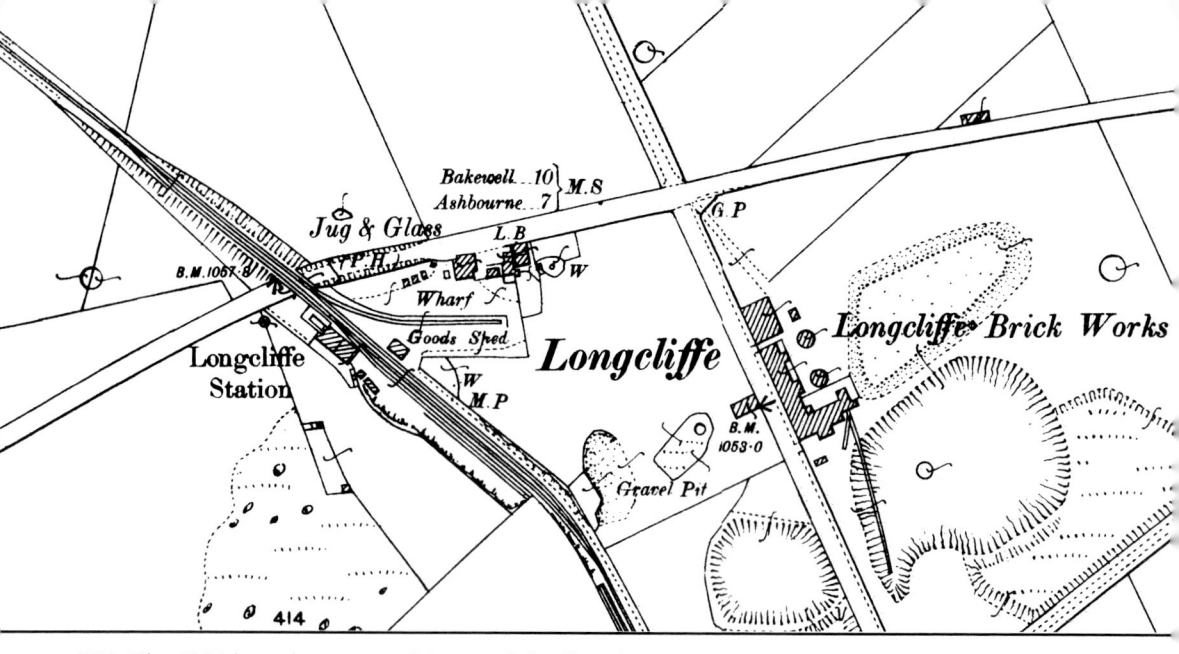

XV. The 1898 issue has many of the usual details. The Jug & Glass is the name of the local public house. The geology varied in this area more than elsewhere.

56. The SLS tour on 25th April 1953 is seen with 0-6-0T no. 58856 blowing off and photographers' cars awaiting an unusually crowded train. (M.J.Stretton coll.)

57. It is some time in 1931 and 2-4-0T no. 6427 is shunting. Listed as 1P, it was produced by the LNWR in July 1876. (Dr J.Hollick/R.Humm coll.)

58. Working the 9.5am Middleton to Friden service on 1st September 1956 is class J94 0-6-0ST no. 68013. This was another wartime engine built for the MOS. (M.Dart coll.)

59. This is an SLS Special on 15th April 1961. It was bound for Middleton Top, having left Parsley Hay at 4.52pm. The loco is 0-6-0ST no. 68013, again. (J.Langford)

MINNINGLOW

XVI. The 1898 edition shows a level crossing which was ungated.

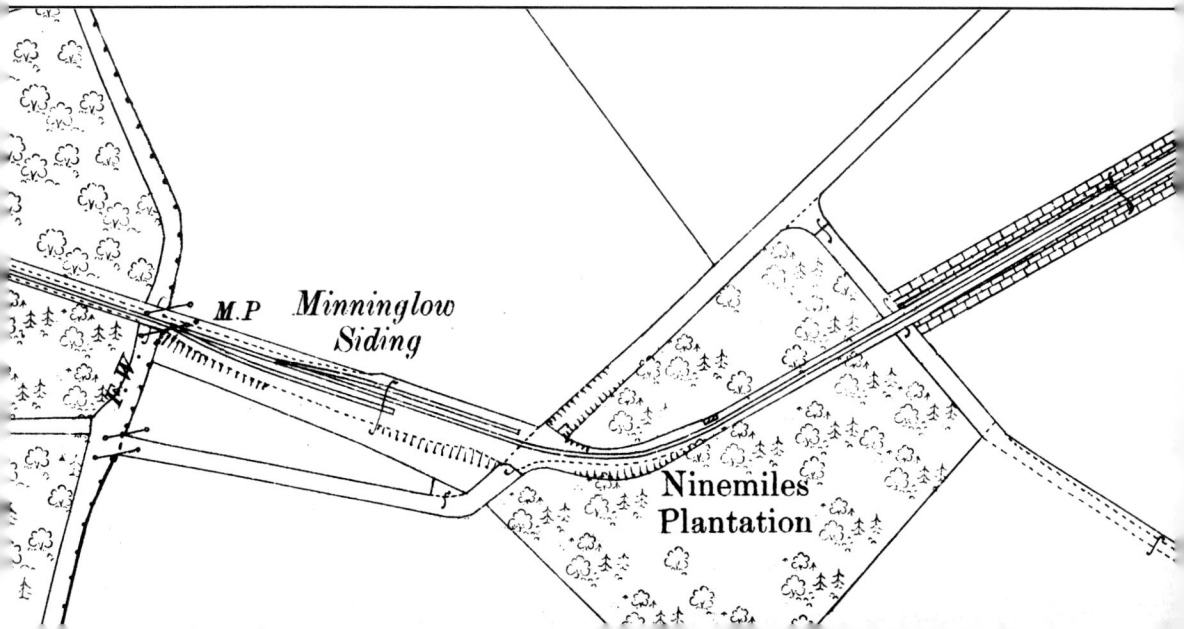

60. A rare view from the guards van on a mixed freight train reveals embankment reinforcement where its height increases greatly. (Bentley coll.)

61. The early sidings here were used for milk traffic, but there is trace of only one in this late view from 2nd April 1965. Drivers were required to stop at locations such as this, to ensure that there was no road traffic imminent. (Bentley coll.)

Gotham Curve

62. The crew pose on their Crewe Goods 2-4-0 no. 3084. It would have been uncomfortable without a cab roof. (R.Humm coll.)

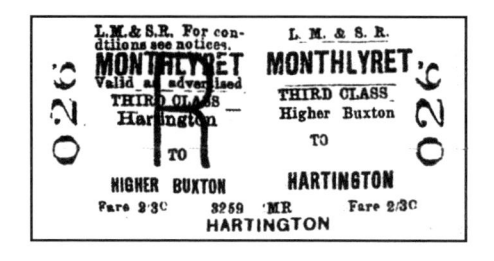

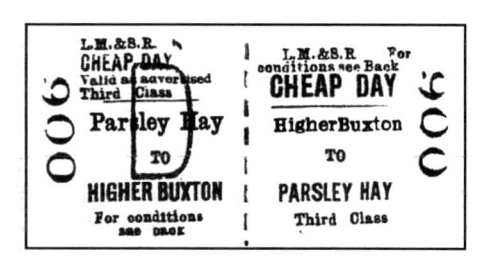

63. We can now enjoy two views from the leading brake van of the SLS Special on 15th April 1961. 0-6-0ST no. 68013 will be squealing against the rusty check rail on the curve. (J.Langford)

64. The formation was three vans and three wagons, but the conversation could seldom be heard with so many iron wheels on steel rails. Iron ore had once been raised in the district. (J.Langford)

65. It is 2nd April 1965 and the firebox of J94 0-6-0ST no. 68079 is receiving fresh coal. At least the fireman was warm. Its superelevation was considerable and its radius 55yds. (Bentley coll.)

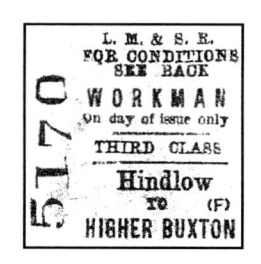

Newhaven Road

66. Gates are across the road on 25th September 1955, while nos 58860 and 58850 haul an extremely large number of happy admirers. One has abandoned his Ford Consul on the grass. The latter loco was acquired by the Bluebell Railway and it has been fired by your scribe (V.M.) in several Summers. (R.Humm coll.)

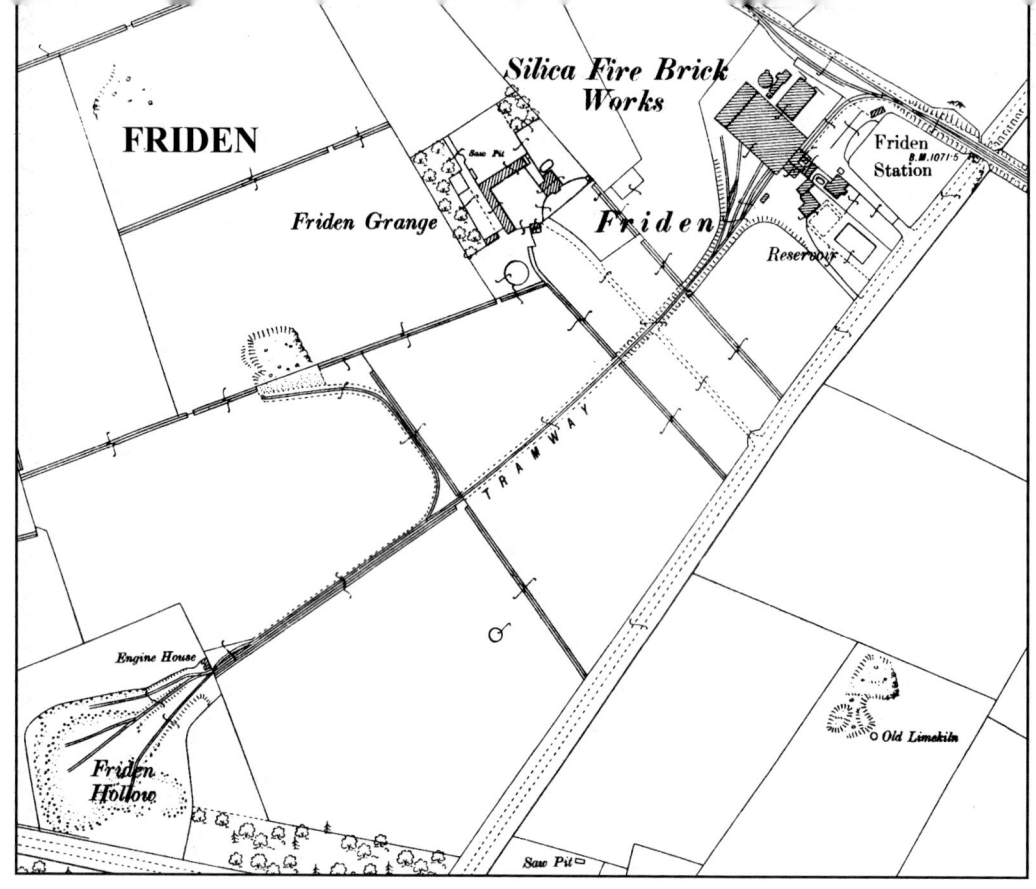

XVII. The 1898 map refers to a station, but there was only a private siding here then. The residents of the adjacent grange might have joined a horse-drawn train here, 50 years earlier. The tramway was later moved nearer to the road, which became the B5056 in 1919.

67. Friden Brickworks had an extensive 2ft gauge railway connecting the pits to the works. Originally horse-worked, a fleet of petrol and diesel locomotives were introduced from 1922. On 24th September 1974, a 1946 30 H.P. Ruston diesel locomotive is seen bringing some Hudson tippers up to the works on the roadside tramway. The C&HPR line crosses over the road bridge in the background. (A.Neale coll.)

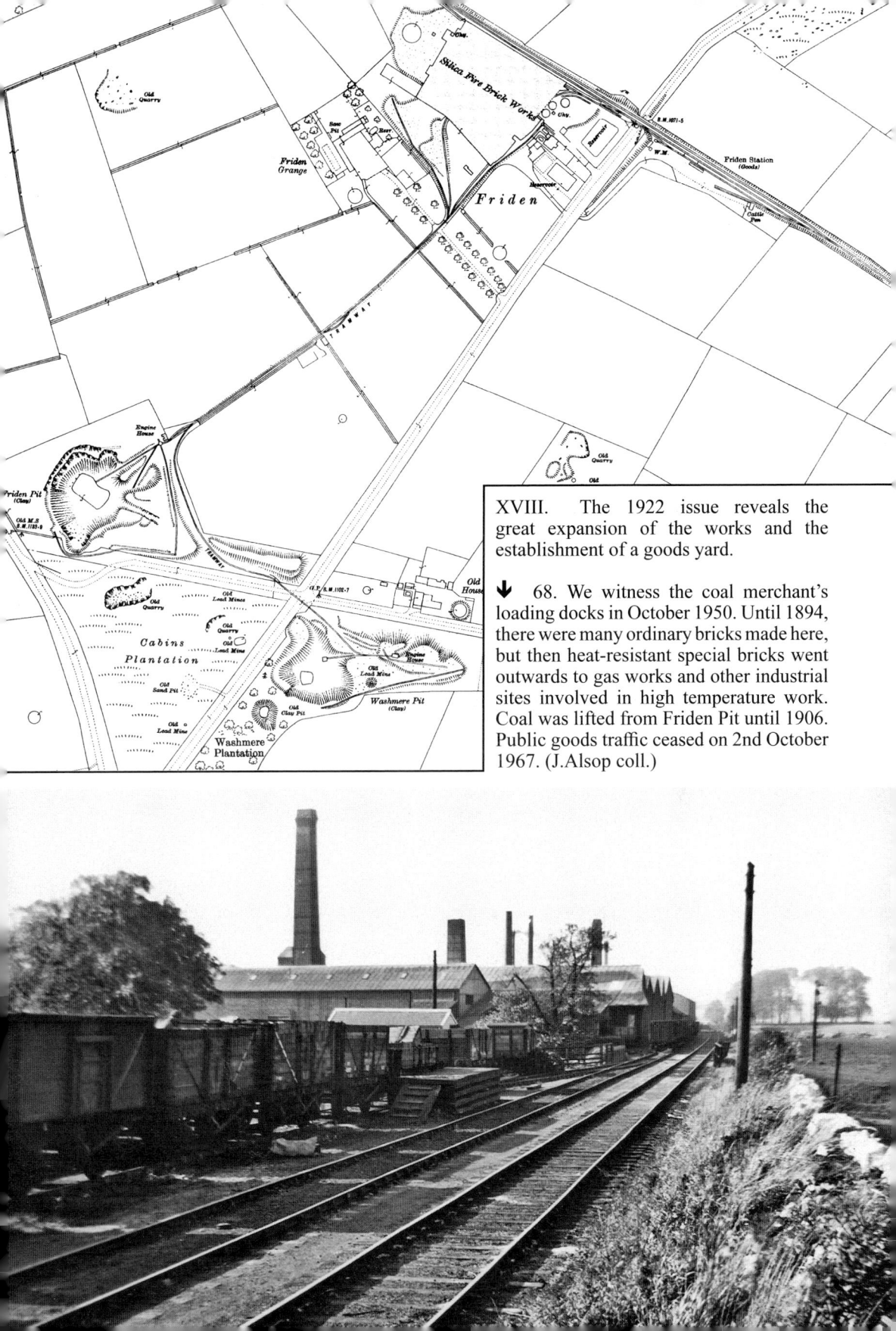

XVIII. The 1922 issue reveals the great expansion of the works and the establishment of a goods yard.

⬇ 68. We witness the coal merchant's loading docks in October 1950. Until 1894, there were many ordinary bricks made here, but then heat-resistant special bricks went outwards to gas works and other industrial sites involved in high temperature work. Coal was lifted from Friden Pit until 1906. Public goods traffic ceased on 2nd October 1967. (J.Alsop coll.)

Blakemoor Siding

69. The pit here raised coal from 1906, but much of it contained pebbles and thus had a limited market, mostly in industry. Some also had clay in it. This 1932 view includes a former loading site. It had just one siding. (Dr J.Hollick/R.Humm coll.)

SOUTH OF PARSLEY HAY

70. The east end of Newhaven Tunnel was photographed in May 1953. The plaque above the portal was dedicated to 'Jos Jessop Esq. Engineer'. (J.Alsop coll)

71. The plaque was still evident on 21st July 1982 and had been enjoyed by Peak Trail users since 1968. The path was still offset from the centre line. (Colour-Rail.com)

72. This fine panorama is from 7th April 1959 and shows the divergence of the tracks: left to Cromford and right to Ashbourne. Both lines closed totally in 1967. (E.R.Morton/J.Suter coll.)

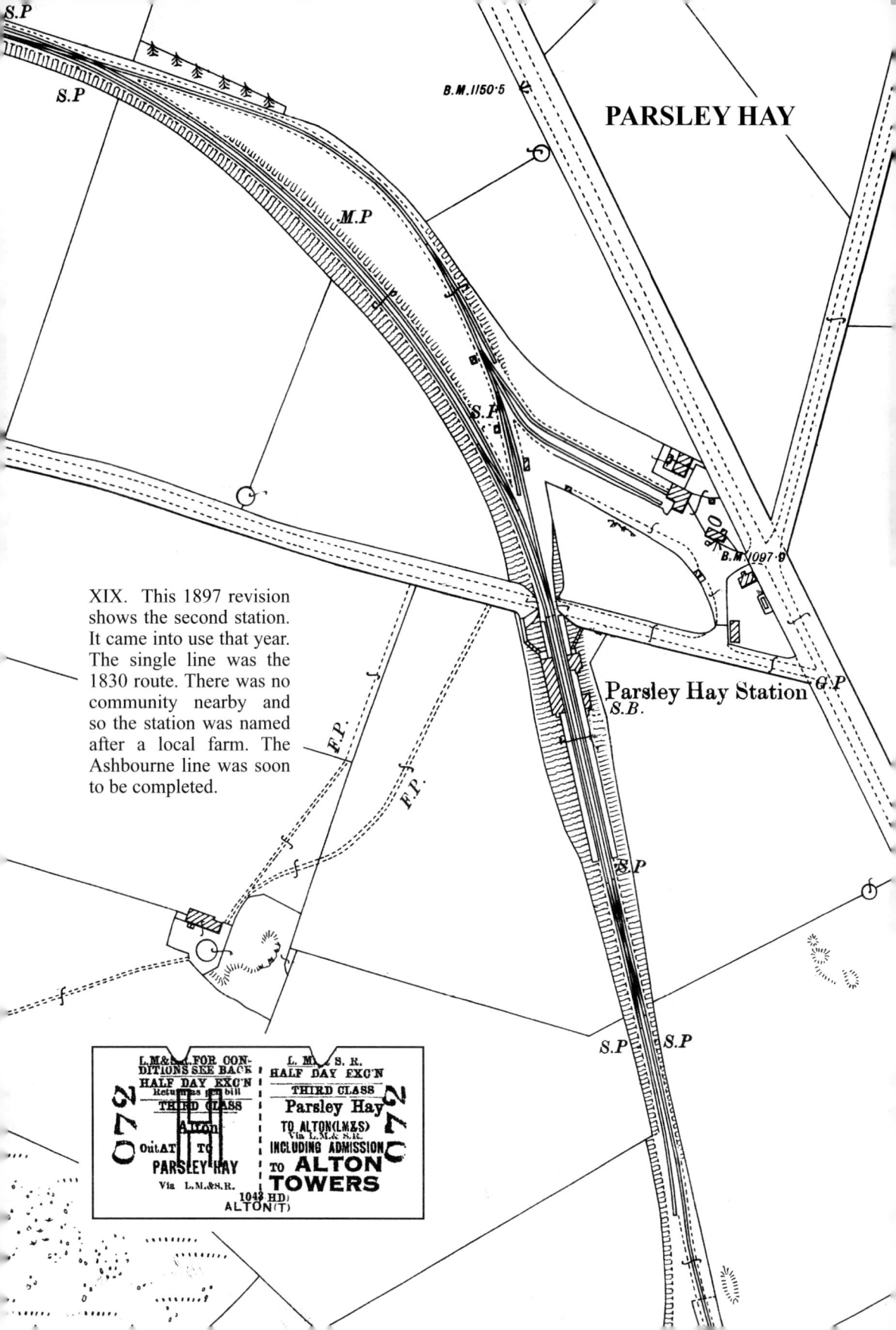

PARSLEY HAY

XIX. This 1897 revision shows the second station. It came into use that year. The single line was the 1830 route. There was no community nearby and so the station was named after a local farm. The Ashbourne line was soon to be completed.

73. A view north in 1932 includes the curves which served the original terminus and later the goods yard. The former was in use in 1894-99 and the latter until 6th July 1964. (R.S.Carpenter coll.)

74. We are still looking north, with the yard and its 5-ton crane jib in the distance. The sloping roof and ventilators on the left were for the benefit of gentlemen. The picture was taken in October 1954. (J.Suter coll.)

75. This wide panorama is from 1960 and reveals the extensive supports required. The stairs made a long climb up from the road, but no subway was ever provided, as there were few passengers here. (Colour-Rail.com)

76. This SLS tour on 15th April 1961 has just arrived behind a class J94 0-6-0ST. There are elbows galore. Regular passenger service had ceased here on 1st November 1954. (D.Lawrence/Photos from the Fifties)

77. Class 7F 0-8-0 no. 49262 is seen on 14th June 1962. The signalman was the only member of staff here by that time. They were authorised to obtain coal for their stove from waiting engines; a nice task in June. (Colour-Rail.com)

78. All the station structures were demolished in 1966, except for the 1894 signal box, which had 36 levers. It was closed on 25th October 1967, along with the line northwards. The tiny building was provided following the loss of the station toilets. Water was provided in the milk churns. (A.F.Bullimore)

79. Parsley Hay cycle hire centre brought new opportunities for enjoyable transport in this High Peak area. (© Peak District National Park Authority)

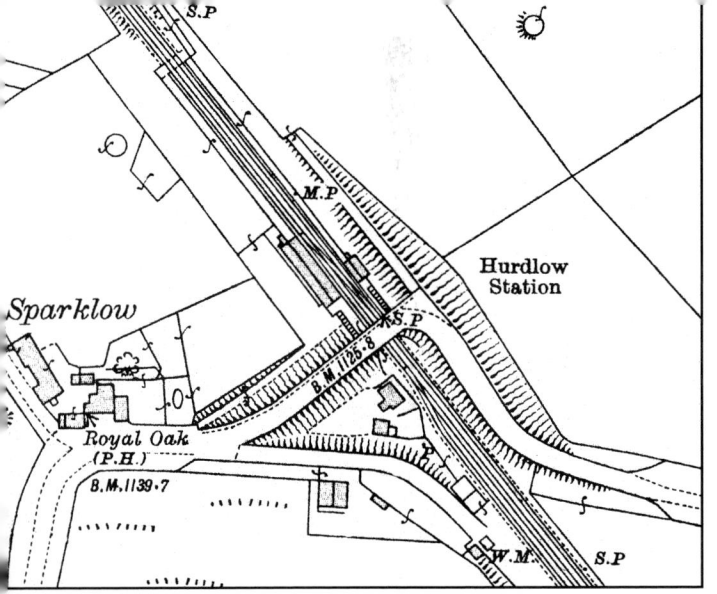

HURDLOW

XX. A goods service was provided here from 1833 and passengers in 1856-77. It was restored in 1894 and this map is from 1897.

↓ 80. Following the realignment of the C&HPR route, the running lines were on the bridge in this 1932 photo. The lane is the back road to Hartington. Until 1869, there had been an 850yd long incline near here, graded at 1 in 16.
(R.Humm coll.)

↓ 81. This view south is from May 1953, although the station had closed on 15th August 1949. There were very few residents nearby. Much of the fencing has been used elsewhere. Further north was Dowlow Halt, which was opened to the public in 1929-54. Its stark appearance can be found in *Uttoxeter to Buxton*. (J.Alsop coll.)

Briggs Siding

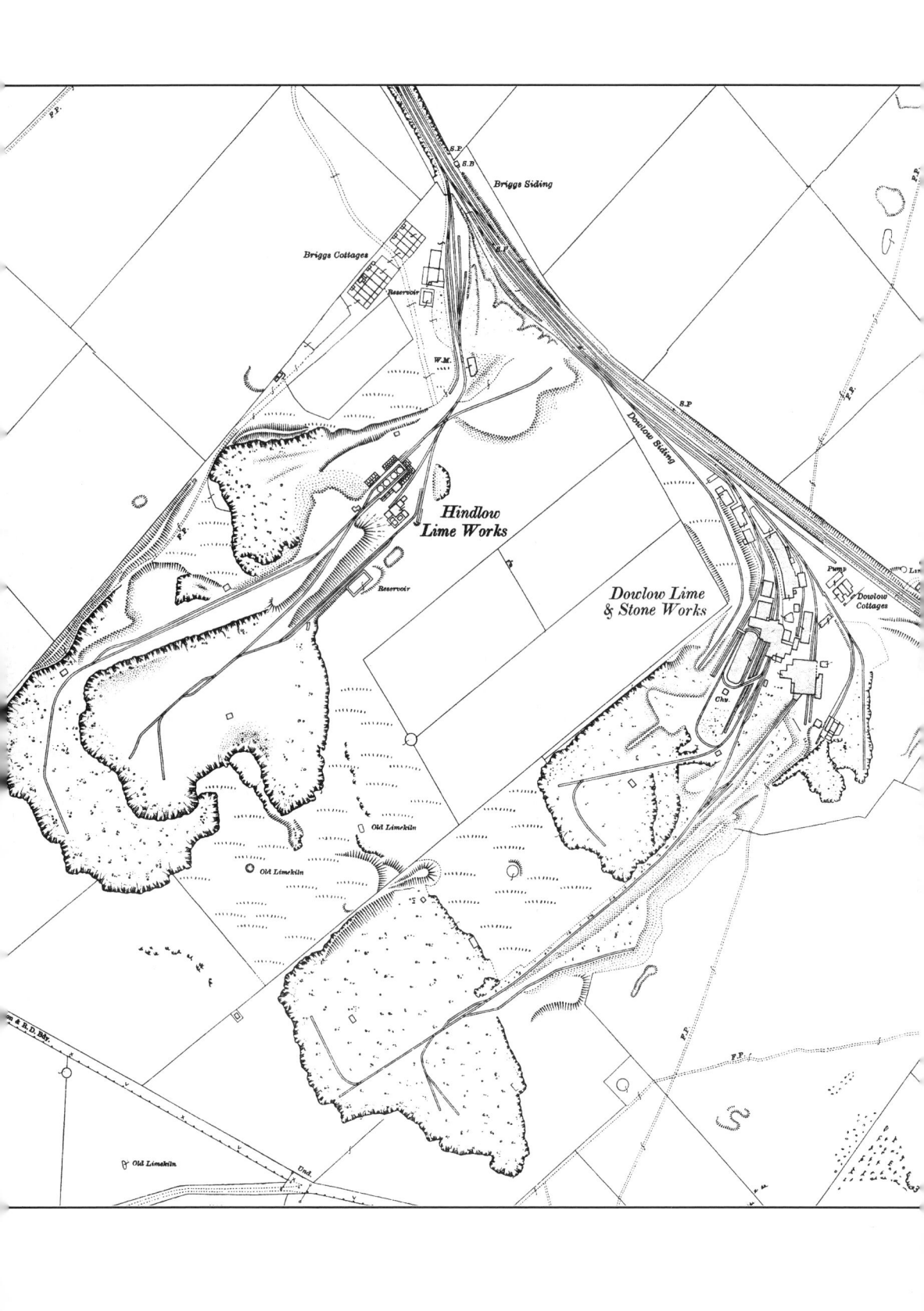

Briggs Cottages

Reservoir

Hindlow
Lime Works

Dowlow Siding

Dowlow Lime
& Stone Works

Dowlow Cottages

Old Limekiln

Old Limekiln

← XXI. The 1922 issue indicates the great extent of the works at that time. It grew steadily over the fields eastwards, subsequently.

82. No. 47068 departs from Hindlow with the daily trip working from Hindlow to Ashburys on 10th April 1984, conveying one PBA covered hopper wagon with lime for Barnby Dun glassworks. At that time, Hindlow dispatched wagonloads of lime to Barnby Dun and Mossend, using the Speedlink network. The last vacuum-braked open wagons had given way to air-braked covered hoppers in the previous year. (P.D.Shannon)

83. Beswicks Lime Works Ltd at Hindlow was the first major customer for Hudswell Clarke-built diesel locomotives, buying two standard gauge and four 2ft gauge locomotives between 1930 and 1936. One of each of the 2ft gauge types were photographed in the quarry on 5th April 1969. This is no. 3 (Hudswell D564), a 30 H.P. locomotive built in 1930 (S.A.Leleux/A.Neale coll.)

84. This picture shows a smaller 20 H.P. locomotive (Hudswell D589), which was supplied in 1936. The equipment for loading the tipper wagons is in the background. (S.A.Leleux/A.Neale coll.)

85. This petrol locomotive was built by Crossley Brothers of Manchester in about 1925 and was photographed at Beswicks Lime Works in around 1934. (A.Neale coll.)

86. The narrow gauge system connecting the quarry with the limeworks of T.Ryan Somerville & Co. Ltd at Hindlow was a relatively modern one of 3ft 6ins gauge. It employed four 48 H.P. Ruston & Hornsby diesel locomotives, delivered in May 1944, hauling all steel Hudson side tippers holding 3.5 cubic yds of rock. This view taken in 1948 also shows the supplementary 2ft gauge railway put in about this time. (A.Neale coll.)

HINDLOW

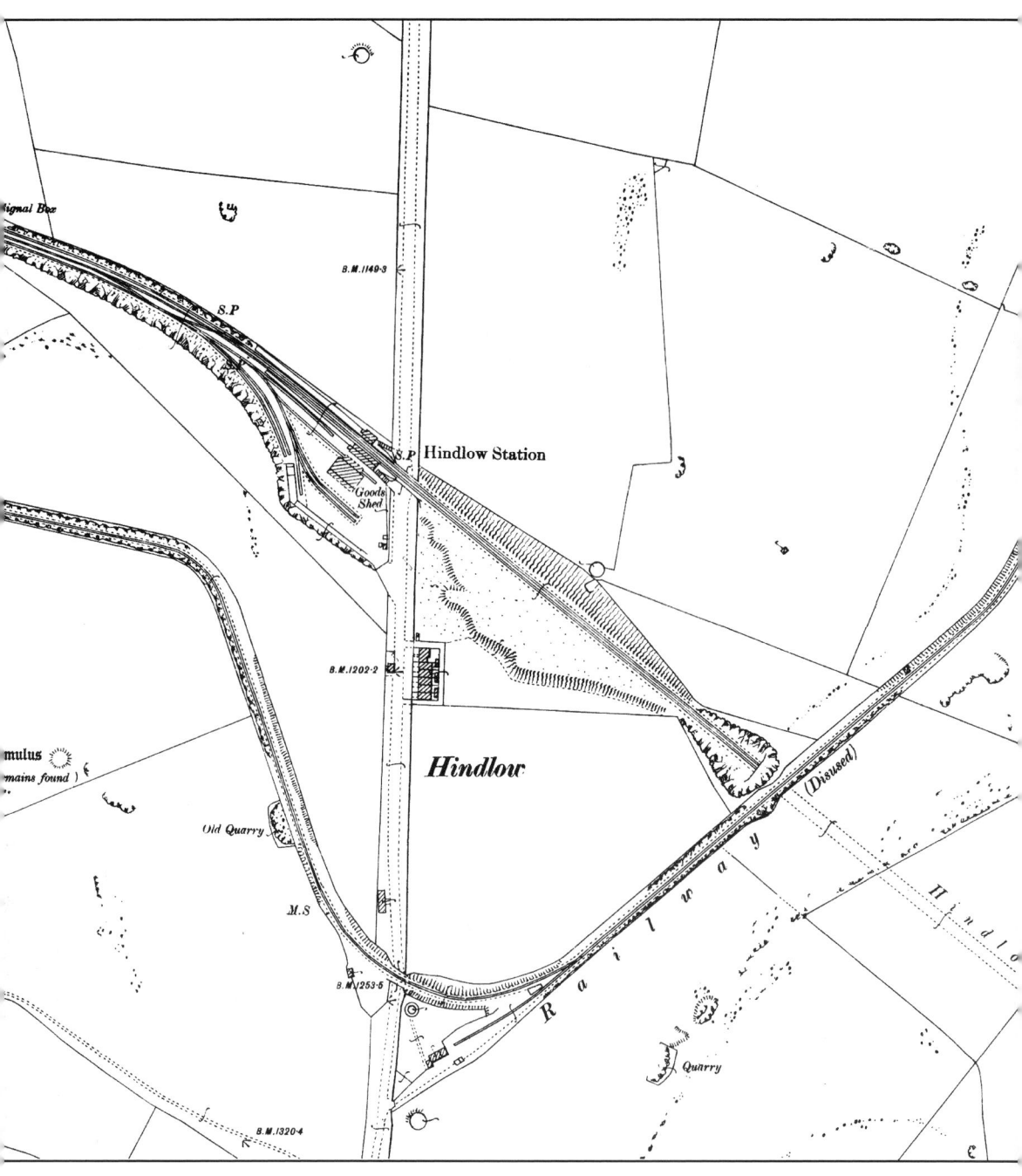

XXII. The 1898 edition has the original C&HPR 1833 route marked as disused. It conveyed some passengers between 1856 and 1877. The diagonal line to Hindlow Tunnel and the station shown was opened by the LNWR on 1st June 1894. The small building at the end of the siding at the bottom of this map was the original station. It had a weighing machine at its southern corner.

87. We are northwest of the station, looking southeast, with Brierlow Lime Works dominating the scene, in the right background. The signal box is north of the station; top left on the map. It closed on 30th June 1982. The goods yard had a 30cwt crane. (J.Suter coll.)

88. The structure of the station was similar to the previous two, being built largely of timber. Closure to regular passenger trains came on 1st November 1954. (SLS coll.)

HARPUR HILL

← 89. Both this and picture 90 were taken in the early 1930s and show the Hoffman Lime kilns, which were served by the Harpur Hill Branch. The very rough narrow gauge trackwork was of 2ft 2½ ins gauge. Standard gauge wagons are being filled with limestone in this view. (A.Neale coll.)

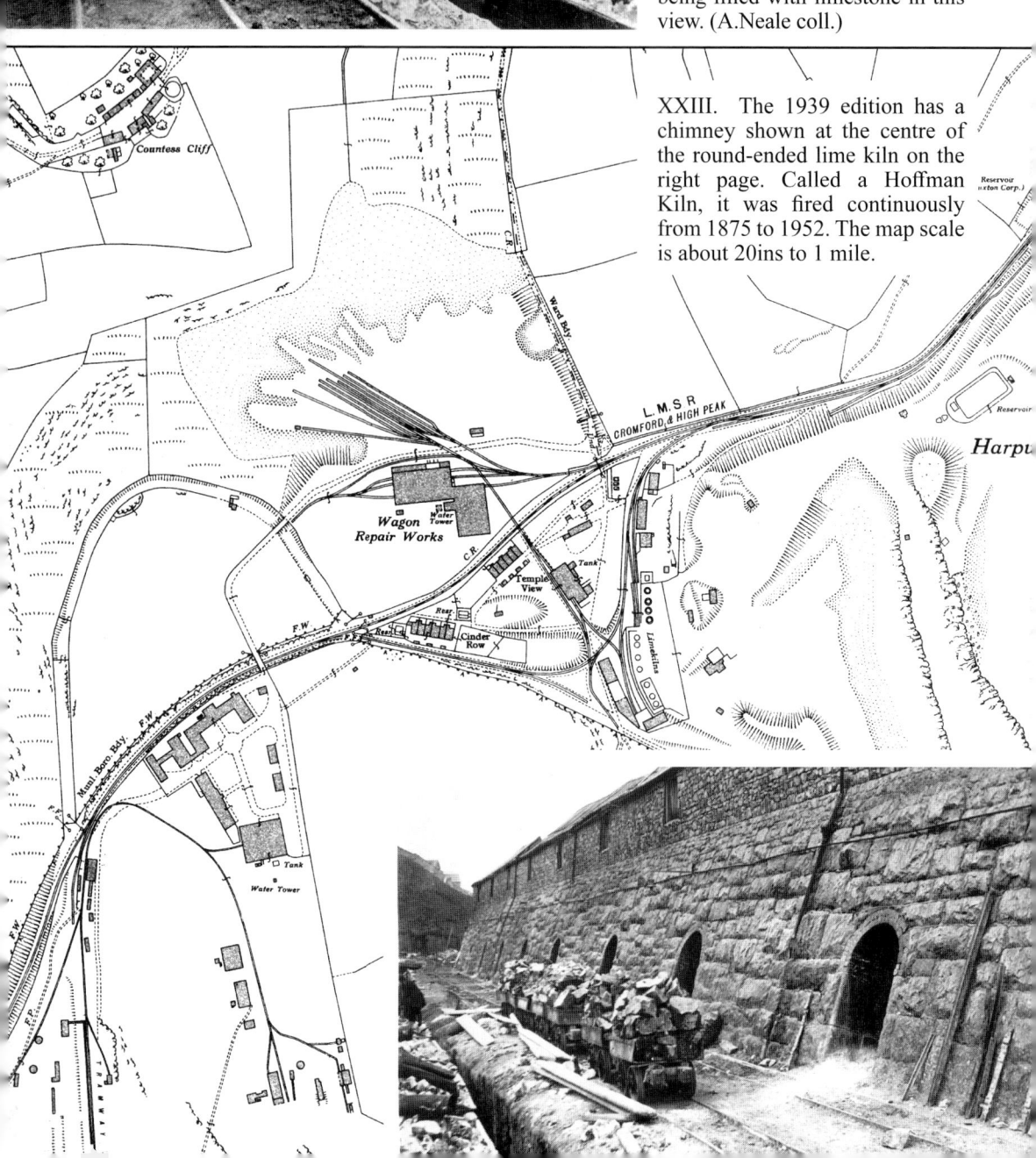

XXIII. The 1939 edition has a chimney shown at the centre of the round-ended lime kiln on the right page. Called a Hoffman Kiln, it was fired continuously from 1875 to 1952. The map scale is about 20ins to 1 mile.

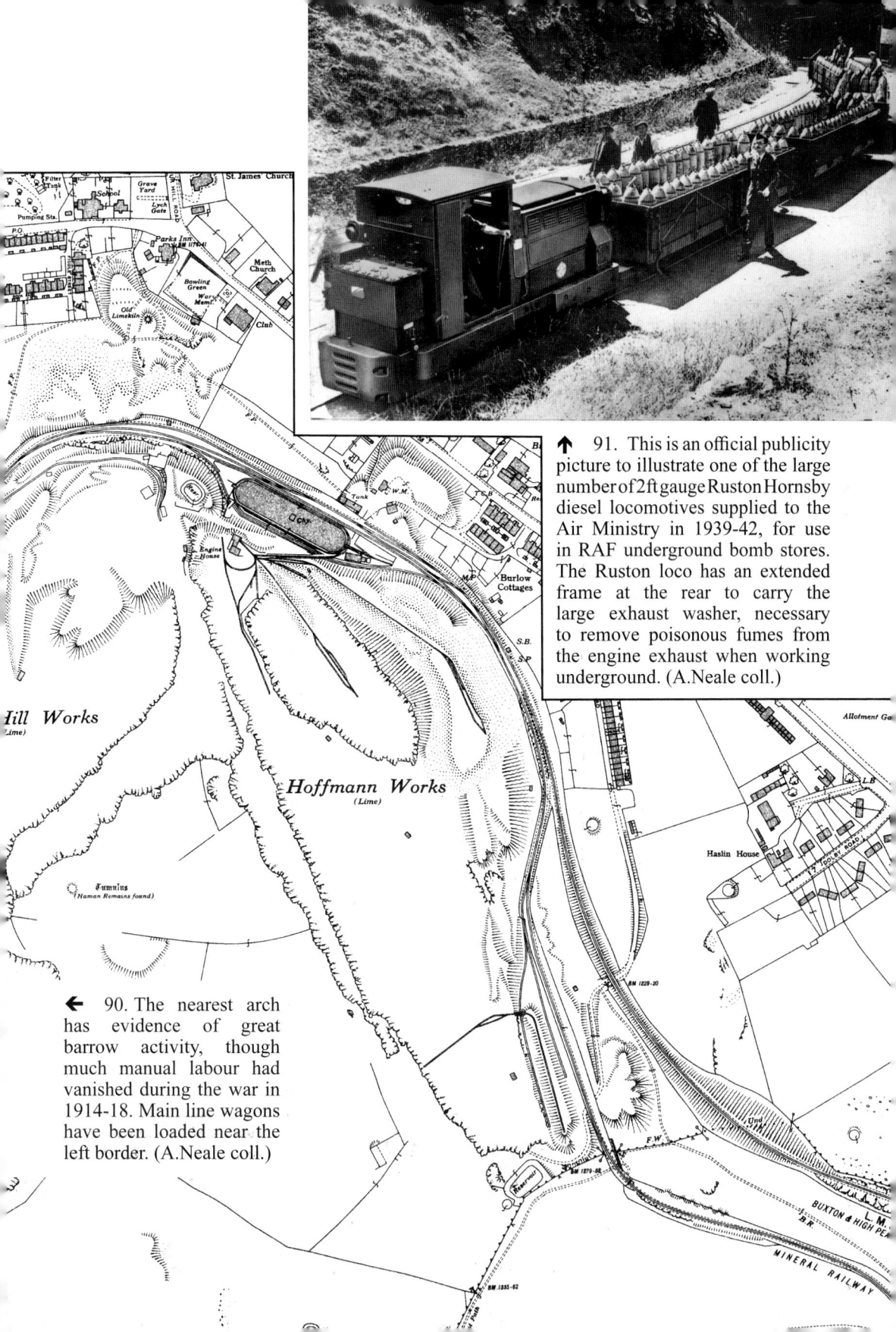

91. This is an official publicity picture to illustrate one of the large number of 2ft gauge Ruston Hornsby diesel locomotives supplied to the Air Ministry in 1939-42, for use in RAF underground bomb stores. The Ruston loco has an extended frame at the rear to carry the large exhaust washer, necessary to remove poisonous fumes from the engine exhaust when working underground. (A.Neale coll.)

90. The nearest arch has evidence of great barrow activity, though much manual labour had vanished during the war in 1914-18. Main line wagons have been loaded near the left border. (A.Neale coll.)

GRIN BRANCH

92. This shows the loco shed at the Clay Cross Co., Grin Quarry, and was taken on 29th December 1946. At the time, the loco shed contained an early Sentinel vertical boilered geared locomotive. (A.Neale coll.)

93. Working in the Grinlow Quarries in 1932 was this 0-6-0ST. It was built by Andrew Barclay and was called *Clyde*. The river of this name flowed near their factory. Grin Works is now a caravan site. (Dr J.Hollick/Bentley coll.)

➜ XXIV. The 1947 edition at 1in to 1 mile has Harpurhill 1½ ins south of the centre of Buxton and Ladmanlow the same distance southwest of it. The route then curves north and ends just before 'Tunnel'. Thereafter, the trackbed is fairly straight to the edge of Whaley Bridge, which is in the top left corner. Between it and the left margin is Toddbrook Reservoir. This was built to supply the Peak Forest Canal but suffered a small dam failure after 200 years, on 1st August 2019, after intense rain.

Bugsworth
Whitehough
Whaley Bridge
Horwich End
Chapel Milton
Slack Hall
Bowden Hall
Stonyford
Bagshaw
Coalpithole Mine
Peaslows
Sparrowpit
CHAPEL EN LE FRITH
Blackbrook
Lower Eaves
Eaves
Bennetston Hall
Bolt Edge
Ebbing & Flowing Well
Barmoor
Bee Low
Lodesbarn
Martinside
Sittinglow
Near Ridgeclose
Cowlow
Hallsteads Top
Bull Ring
Lodes Marsh
Dove Holes
Lime Works
Lower Bibbington
Higher Bibbington
Peak Dale
Smalldale
Springmound
Peak Ho.
Batham Gate
Upper End
Hardybarn
Great Rocks Pastures
Orient Lodge
Green Fairfield
Great Rocks Back Pasture
Fairfield
Fairfield Common
Golf Course
Dalehead
Daisymere Fm
Lowfoot
BUXTON
Ashwood Dale
Tim Lodge
Woolow
Pictor Hall
Cowlow
Kingsterndale
The Cottage
Staden
Staden Grange
Cowdale
Earthwork
King's Piece
Heathfield Nook
Haslin Ho.
Staker Hill
Hillhead
Brierlow Bar
Hind Low
Brier Low
Harley
Dow Low
Jericho
Hatchways
Dowel
Chrome
Upper Edge
Dowel Dale
Hollins Hill
Fough
Booth
Stoop
High Edge
Greensides
Harpur Hill
Countess Cliff
Anthony Hill
Grin Low
Grin Plant
Solomon's Temple
Ladmanlow
Stanley Moor
Burbage
Burbage Edge
Shay Lodge
Edgemoor
Corbar Hill
Lightwood Reservoirs
Flint Clough
Combs Moss
Combs Edge
Black Edge
Brown Edge
White Hall
Long Hill
Hanging Rock
Combs
Combs Reservoir
Wild Moor
HARTINGTON UPPER QUARTER
Goyt's Moss
Raven's Low
Stake Side
Goytsclough
Derbyshire Br.
Moss Ho.
Old Coal Pits
Axe Edge Moor
Axe Edge
Cheeks Hill
Colliery
Danebower Quarries
Dane Colliery
Blackclough
Three Shire Heads
Knotbury
Dove Head
Axe Edge End
Brand Side
Brand Top
Brand End
Dalehead
Leap Edge
Turncliff
Thirkelow
Hawk's Nest
Turn Edge
Wolf Edge
Oliver Hill
New Lodge
Head of River Manifold
Colshaw
Summerhill
Saltswell
Tenterhill
Washgate
Fernilee
Errwood
Goyt's Br.
Goytsbridge
Hill Top
Tunstead
Cockyard
Bradshaw Hall
Sparkbottom
Eccles Ho.
Lidgate
Burrfields
Shallcross Manor
Oldfield
Wythen Lache
Pygreave
Allstone Lee
Broadlee Fm
Rake End
Bunsal Fm
Moss Chain
Whetstone Ridge
Danebower Hollow

LADMANLOW

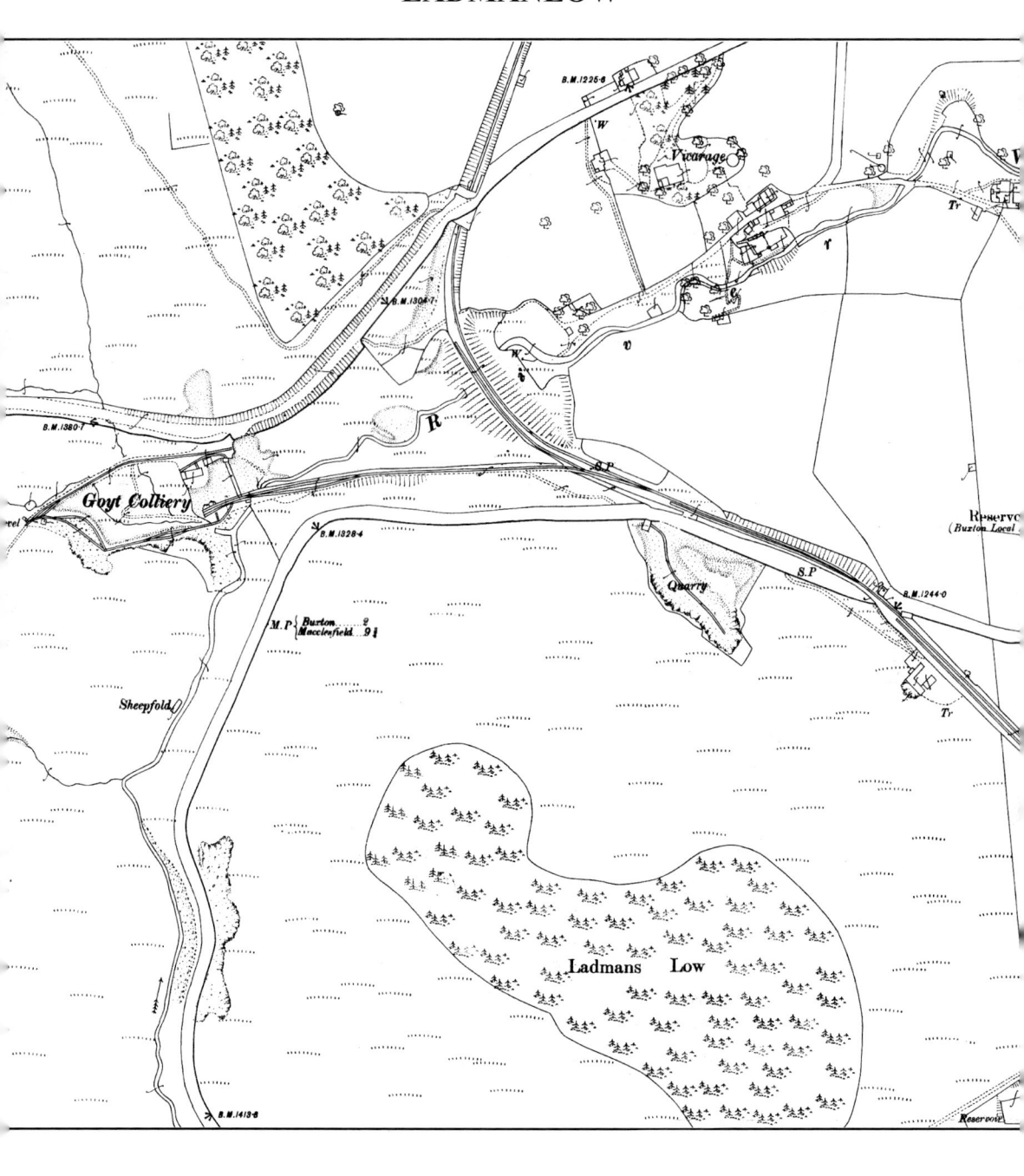

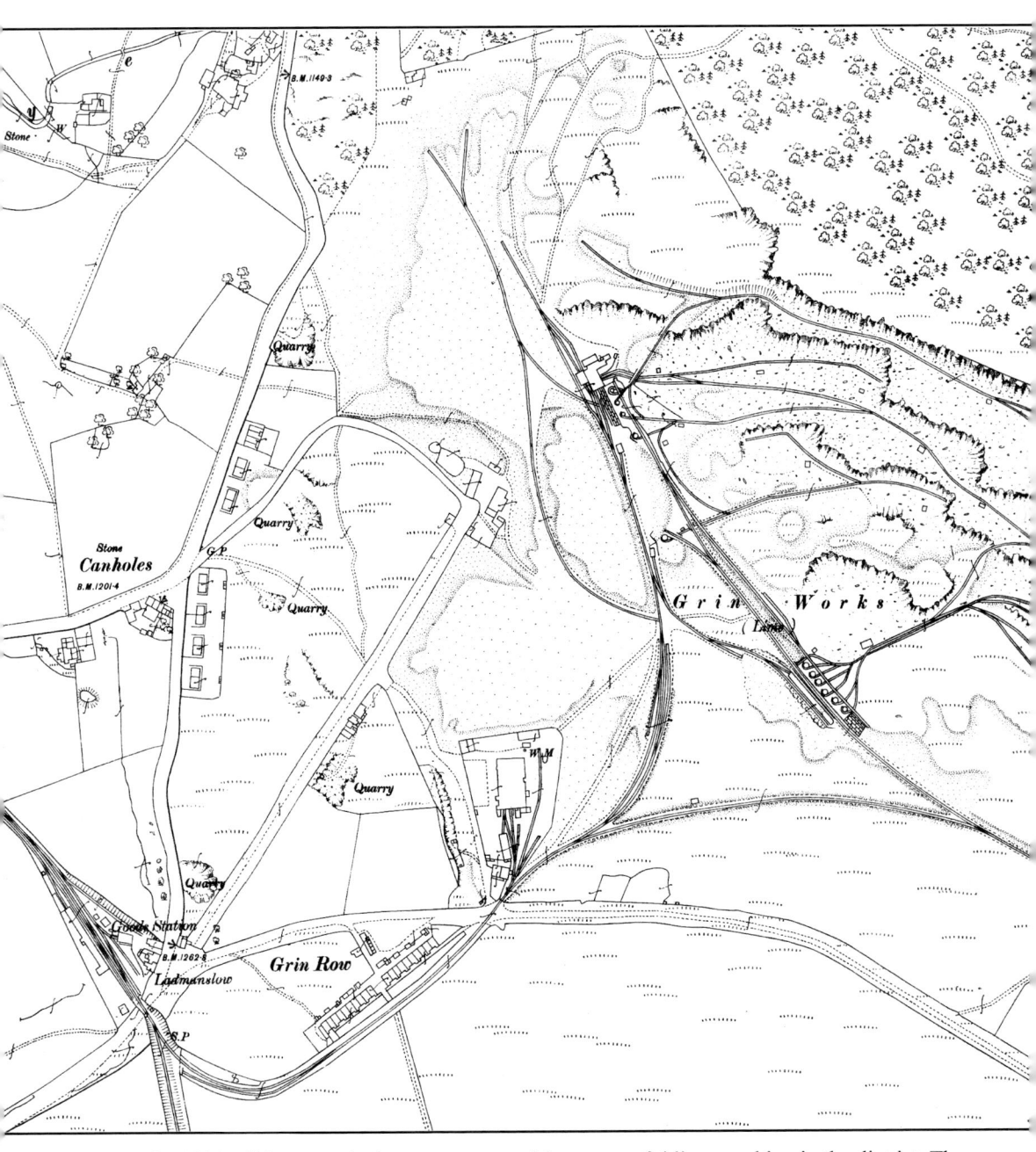

XXV. The 1880 edition reveals the great extent of the successful lime working in the district. The station can be found lower left on the right page.

94. This view south, with the Leek Road (A53) level crossing gates in the distance, is from 1932. The signal post carries an arm for both directions. They were presumably operated by the gatekeeper. There were no signal boxes in this area. Control was thus: Hindlow to Harpur Hill, Train Staff & Ticket; Harpur Hill to Old Harpur, Siding working and Old Harpur to Ladmanlow, Train Staff. (J.Alsop coll.)

95. Here we look north from the A53 in 1932 and see most of the goods yard. It was in use until 1954. The small gate could be used under staff supervision if the large ones had prolonged closure; it was known as a wicket gate. The poster is promoting a trip to Blackpool. (R.Humm coll.)

NORTH OF LADMANLOW

96. We are less than ½ mile from the station in 1932, looking at the Old Macclesfield Road bridge. The track north of here closed in 1892 and southwards in 1954. (R.Humm coll.)

Burbage Tunnel

97. The high ground surrounds the north end of the boarded-up north tunnel mouth in 1932. The farm track turns left, up the hill. (R.Humm coll.)

98. The Bunsall Incline had been in two parts, 660 and 450 yds in length, with gradients of 1 in 7½ and 1 in 7, respectively. The two were combined operationally in 1857 and abandoned in 1892, when the line closed. (Bentley coll.)

Goyt Valley

99. Fernilee Reservoir in the Goyt Valley was built by Lehane, McKenzie & Shand Ltd of Derby between February 1932 and June 1937. They employed 15 3ft gauge steam locos, almost all of which were transferred from their previous contract of building Gorple Reservoir for Halifax Corporation. They also used two 2ft gauge steam stock, which ran on a temporary line along the trackbed of the former C&HPR Ladmanlow to Shallcross line that closed in 1892. The 3ft gauge Hunslet 0-4-0ST *Brownhill* (Hunslet 32 of 1903) is in the yard at Fernilee in April 1933. Note the massive dumb buffers for shunting the wooden tipping wagons. (A.Neale coll.)

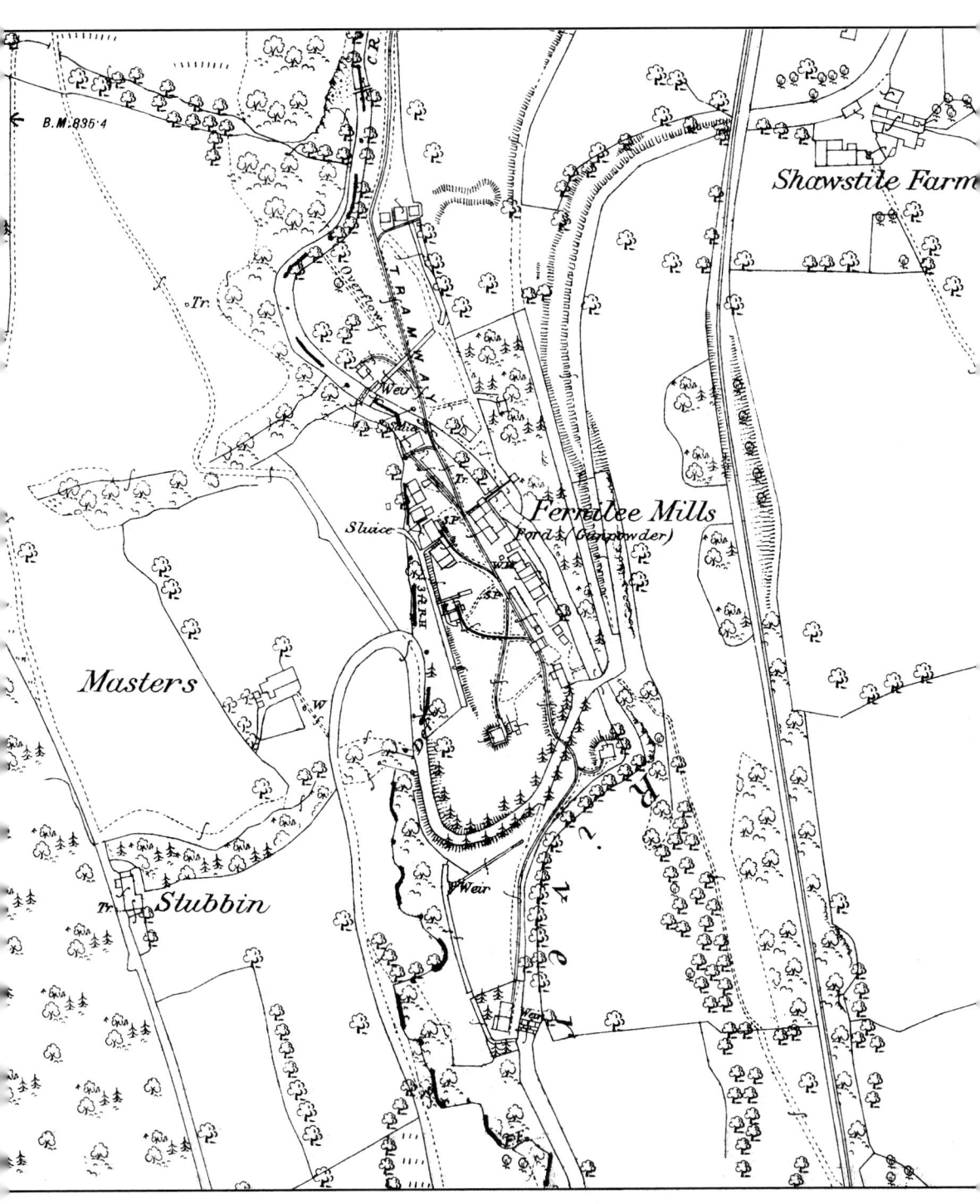

XXVI. This 1885 map has the word gunpowder under the mill's name. This was before World Wars banned such revelations. The line top centre continued to the Magazine. Production ceased here in 1920 and a reservoir construction over the site began in 1932.

100. Photographed at Fernilee, *Kinder* was a large 0-4-0WT built by Orenstein & Koppel for the Lehane's Gorple Reservoir job. A 12ins diameter water main was laid along the C&HPR trackbed. (A.Neale coll.)

101. This Kerr Stuart 'Wren' 0-4-0ST (KS 3114 of 1918) was one of two 2ft gauge steam locos used at Fernilee during the creation of the massive reservoir. The dam foundations were complete by the end of 1933 and it opened in June 1937. The name was changed to Stockport Reservoir, as it served that town. (A.Neale coll.)

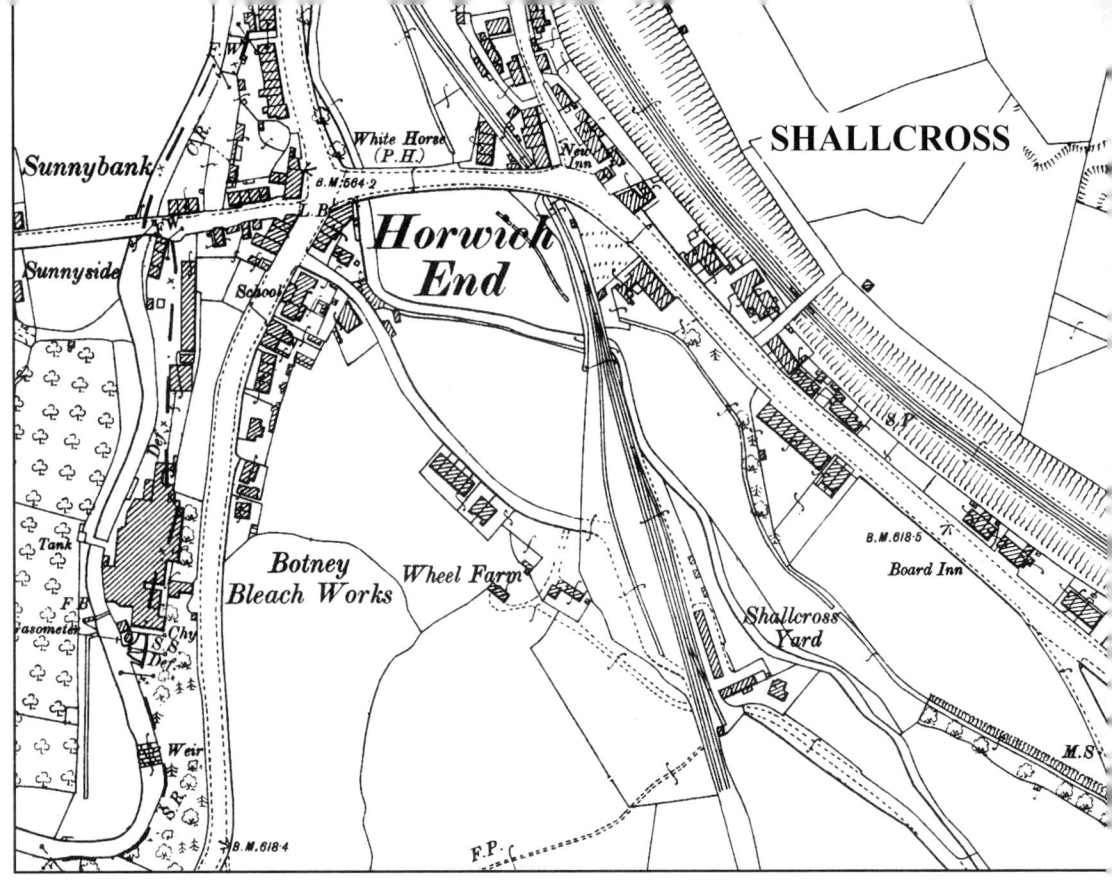

XXVII. Horwich End was the name applied to this southern part of Whaley Bridge. Shallcross was the name used by the C&HPR, whose line terminates near the lower border of the 1898 map. It had done so since 1892. LNWR trains from Buxton used the route curving on the right.

102. This complex glimpse had no details recorded. The heated hut on the left was for the benefit of the shunter. A single line served Shallcross Yard, which is at the bottom of map XXVII. The yard had a 5-ton crane. The Shallcross Incline had been abandoned with the line in 1892. It was 817yds long, at 1 in 10¼. The coaching stock was for the Whaley Bridge to Manchester service. (R.Humm coll.)

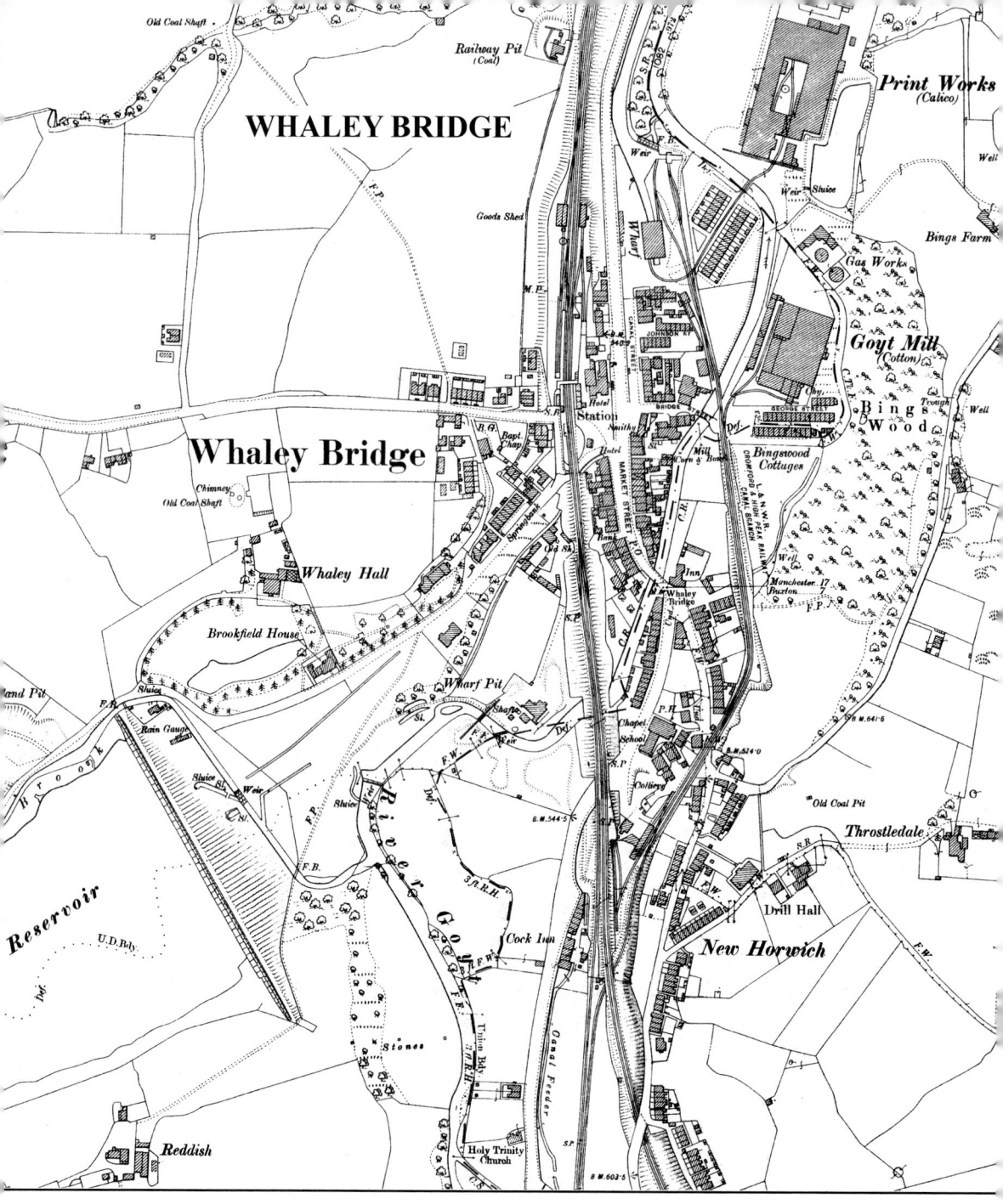

XXVIII. The dam of Toddbrook Reservoir is lower left and its canal feeder is largely underground to the wharf, which is top right. The dam became headline news, after about 200 years, when it developed a defect on 1st August 2019 and residents had to be evacuated in case a total collapse took place. The train service between Buxton and Stockport was suspended from 2nd to 7th August due to the threat. Repairs were successful. Near the lower border of this 1899 issue is another small canal feeder, to the right of which is the C&HPR. It has just become two single tracks, the right one running under the LNWR main line and the left one joining it. Top centre is a pit with a loop adjustment . The River Goyt is shown flowing from lower centre to the top.

103. The bridge was suitable for horse power and the board warns against using engines under it. The early locos had cleared the structure. The direct connection to the main line from the C&HP is on the left. (R.Humm coll.)

104. This was the shortest incline on the route at 180yds long. Its gradient was 1 in 13½ and we are looking north on 10th May 1950. A horse-gin and chains were used until closure on 9th April 1952; the working was counter balanced. (R.Humm coll.)

↓ 105. This was the scene at the bottom of the incline. The granite cobblestones were rounded and thus well-suited for the impact of horseshoes. (R.Humm coll.)

106. The terminus is annotated 'Wharf' near the top of map XXVIII. The canal boats entered the centre of the building's north end, near 'Wear'. At its south end is seen the railway passing through the left doorway. The right one was for road traffic. The transit shed is found in 1949, bearing a notice for START MOTOR Co. It is listed and thus still in place. (R.Humm coll.)

> **For views of the main station, see the Middleton Press album *Buxton to Stockport*, picture nos 71 to 75.**

107. The north end of the wharf was recorded in 1967, with the canal entering the warehouse through a flat top doorway. We have found no evidence of where passengers left their train from Cromford, but it must have been a spectacular journey. (T.Broome)

STEEPLE GRANGE LIGHT RAILWAY

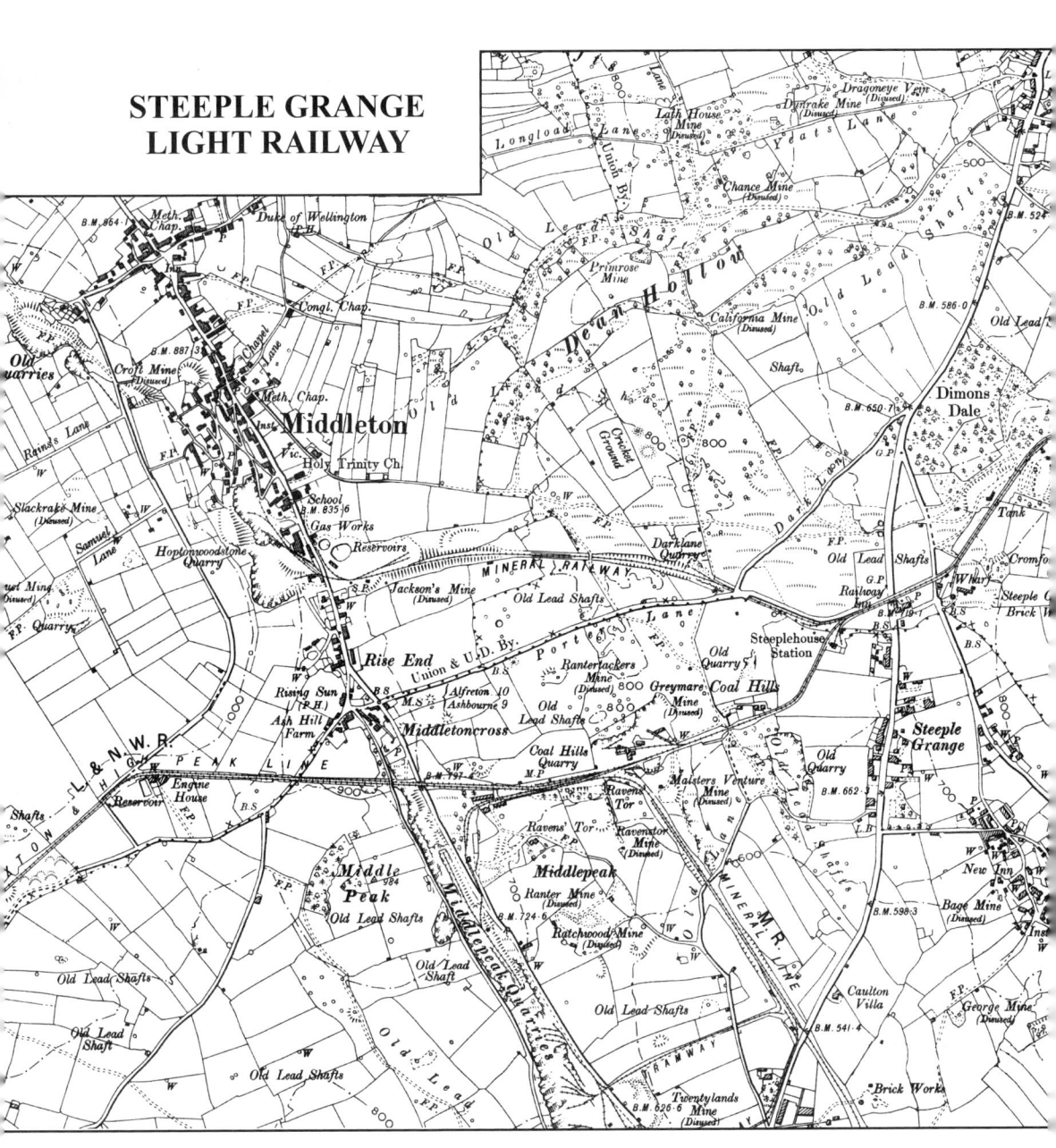

XXIX. We start with an early map to give an understanding of the area in which the Steeple Grange Light Railway was created. This is the 1892 edition at 6ins to 1 mile, with C&HPR from right to left and the connection to the MR lower right. The Steeple Grange line was built along the 1883 track marked MINERAL RAILWAY (centre) from 'Railway Inn' to 'Jackson's Mine'. It was known as Middleton Siding and served Middleton Quarry from 1884 until 1967. It was also known as the 'Killer's Branch'. It had been owned by the Killer brothers.

Our *Branch Line to Wirksworth* **illustrates the route southwards.**

DARK LANE QUARRY
CARRIAGE & WAGON SHED

SANDY LANE
LEVEL CROSSING

RECREATION
GROUND HALT

B5023

PRESTON END
(FOR MIDDLETON)

LAWSON'S LOOP

DARK LANE
QUARRY HALT

RECREATION
GROUND BRIDGE

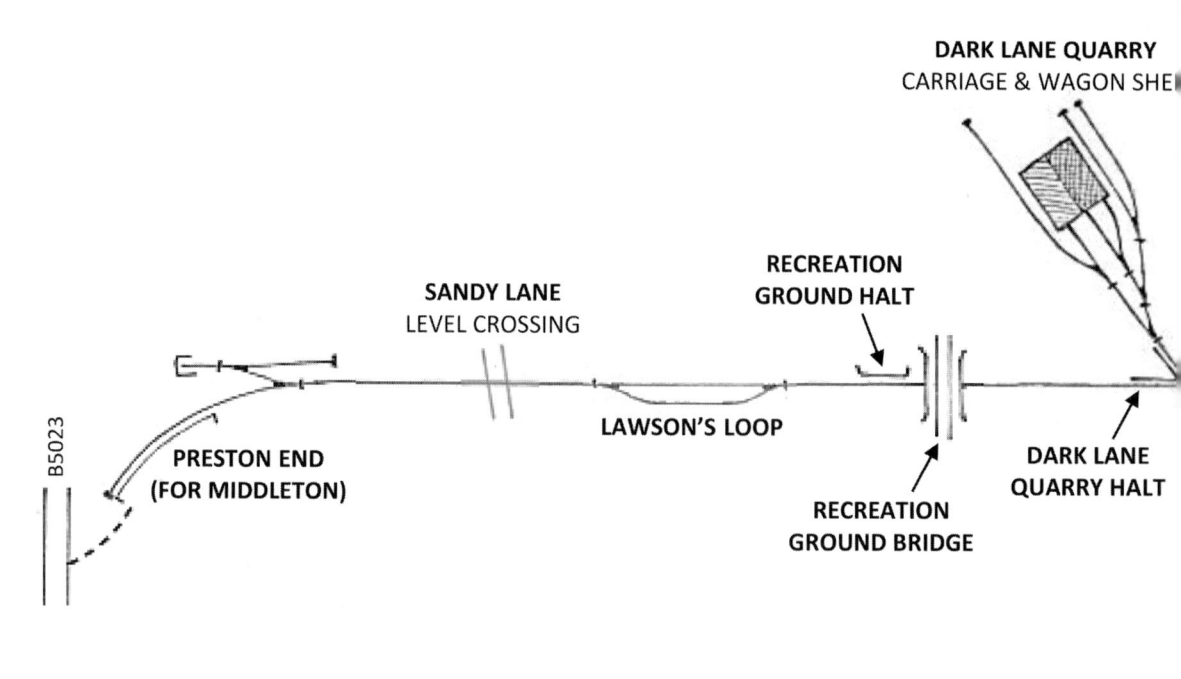

XXX. SGLR track plan in August 2019. (T.Dalton)

108. The most easterly point of the SGLR is Steeplehouse station and the main line headshunt. On the right is the branch line platform that serves Steeplehouse Quarry. Battery electric locomotive *Peggy* (Clayton, B0109B of 1973) is with manrider nos 101 and 102 (ex-Ladywash Mine, Derbyshire) and a new build brake van on an old chassis. (T.Dalton)

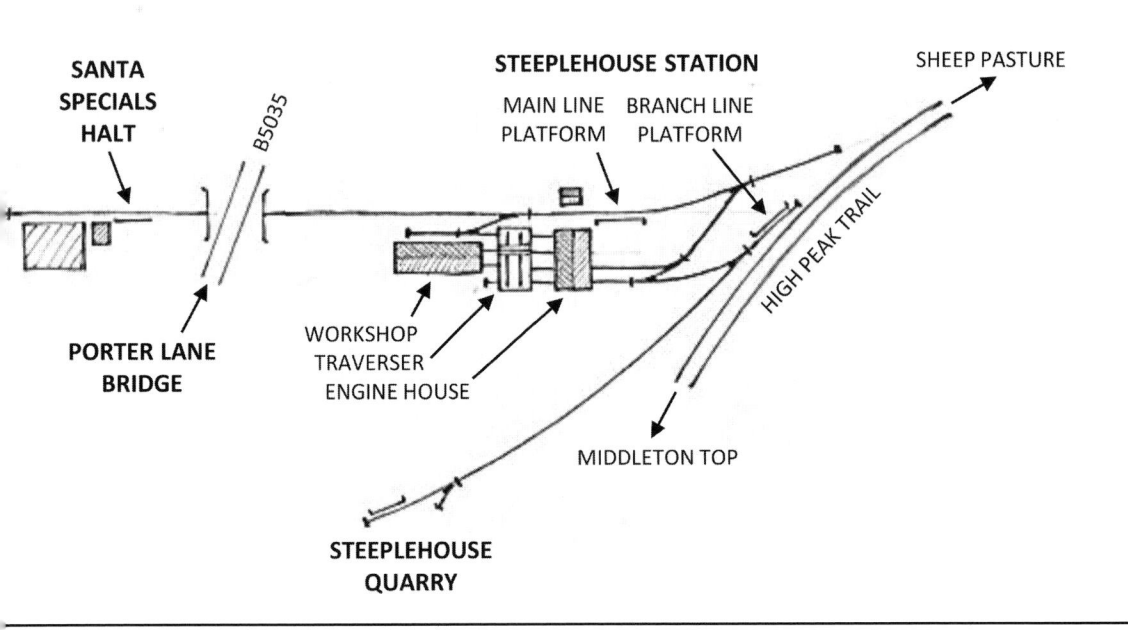

```
SANTA                    STEEPLEHOUSE STATION        SHEEP PASTURE
SPECIALS        B5035    MAIN LINE   BRANCH LINE
HALT                     PLATFORM    PLATFORM

PORTER LANE                                          HIGH PEAK TRAIL
BRIDGE          WORKSHOP
                TRAVERSER
                ENGINE HOUSE
                                     MIDDLETON TOP

                STEEPLEHOUSE
                QUARRY
```

109. Next we see the Engine House, which contains the ticket office, shop and battery charging equipment. Adjacent is the main line platform. Diesel locomotive ZM32 (Ruston & Hornsby, 416214 of 1957) is seen with manrider no. 104 (ex-Bevercotes Colliery, Nottinghamshire). On the right is FC Hibberd 4wPM locomotive 1881 of 1934. (T.Dalton)

110. At the rear of the Engine House is the traverser and new museum/workshop building. Just here the main line begins its ascent westwards. There were 11 locomotives on site in 2019. (T.Dalton)

111. Now we can see the traverser in more detail and also the remainder of the massive stone wall. Its earlier story probably involved laying fresh rails. (T.Dalton)

112. Beyond Porter Lane Bridge is Dark Lane Quarry and the Carriage & Wagon Shed. Note the unusual point into the quarry. (T.Dalton)

113. Just as the climb eases, the main line passes under a charming bridge and into Recreation Ground Halt. (T.Dalton)

114. Further west is 'Lawson's Loop' and ZM32 *Horwich* is seen propelling manrider no. 104 westwards. The ballast is still at a low level. This is the line's most famous engine, a little diesel named after the BR locomotive works in Horwich, Lancashire, where it originally worked. After a spell at Gloddfa Ganol Museum in Blaenau Ffestiniog, *Horwich* came to the SGLR in 1997. (T.Dalton)

STEEPLE GRANGE LIGHT RAILWAY	STEEPLE GRANGE LIGHT RAILWAY
WWW.STEEPLEGRANGE.CO.UK	WWW.STEEPLEGRANGE.CO.UK
1771 **FREE RETURN** 1771	790 **FAMILY RETURN** 790
MAINLINE & BRANCH	MAINLINE & BRANCH
THIS TICKET IS NOT TRANSFERABLE	THIS TICKET IS NOT TRANSFERABLE

115. Continuing along the main line we find ZM32 and manrider no. 104 crossing a private road; the trains must give way to the road traffic here. The train is being safely guided across by the guard. (T.Dalton)

116. The passenger train, ZM32 and manrider no. 104, begins the climb along the new embankment toward the new terminus. (T.Dalton)

For operating days, visit
www.steeplegrange.co.uk
**or telephone
07846 089152.**

← 117. In the distance is the terminus. The train is almost upon the stiffest part of the climb, at 1 in 14. (T.Dalton)

↓ 118. The passenger service reaches the new terminus, the most westerly point of the SGLR. The visitors can stretch their legs whilst a volunteer explains some of the railways' unique history. (T.Dalton)

119. The train negotiates the point work as it enters the new terminus, Preston End. (T.Dalton)

120. The return journey is about to get the 'Right Away'. The guard offers a young visitor the opportunity to wave the green flag. (T.Dalton)

EVOLVING THE

ULTIMATE RAIL ENCYCLOPEDIA

INTERNATIONAL

Easebourne Midhurst GU29 9AZ. Tel:01730 813169

A-978 0 906520 B- 978 1 873793 C- 978 1 901706 D-978 1 904474
E - 978 1 906008 F - 978 1 908174 G - 978 1 910356

Our RAILWAY titles are listed below. Please check availability by looking at our website **www.middletonpress.co.uk**, telephoning us or by requesting a Brochure which includes our LATEST RAILWAY TITLES also our TRAMWAY, TROLLEYBUS, MILITARY and COASTAL series.

email:info@middletonpress.co.uk

A

Abergavenny to Merthyr C 91 8
Abertillery & Ebbw Vale Lines D 84 5
Aberystwyth to Carmarthen E 90 1
Allhallows - Branch Line to A 62 8
Alton - Branch Lines to A 11 6
Ambergate to Buxton G 28 9
Andover to Southampton A 82 6
Ascot - Branch Lines around A 64 2
Ashburton - Branch Line to B 95 4
Ashford - Steam to Eurostar B 67 1
Ashford to Dover A 48 2
Austrian Narrow Gauge D 04 3
Avonmouth - BL around D 42 5
Aylesbury to Rugby D 91 3

B

Baker Street to Uxbridge D 90 6
Bala to Llandudno E 87 1
Banbury to Birmingham D 27 2
Banbury to Cheltenham E 63 5
Bangor to Holyhead F 01 7
Bangor to Portmadoc E 72 7
Barking to Southend C 80 2
Barmouth to Pwllheli E 53 6
Barry - Branch Lines around D 50 0
Bartlow - Branch Lines to F 27 7
Basingstoke to Salisbury A 89 4
Bath Green Park to Bristol C 36 9
Bath to Evercreech Junction A 60 4
Beamish 40 years on rails E94 9
Bedford to Wellingborough D 31 9
Berwick to Drem F 64 2
Berwick to St. Boswells F 75 8
B'ham to Tamworth & Nuneaton F 63 5
Birkenhead to West Kirby F 61 1
Birmingham to Wolverhampton E253
Blackburn to Hellifield F 95 6
Bletchley to Cambridge D 94 4
Bletchley to Rugby E 07 9
Bodmin - Branch Lines around B 83 1
Boston to Lincoln F 80 2
Bournemouth to Evercreech Jn A 46 8
Bournemouth to Weymouth A 57 4
Bradshaw's History F18 5
Bradshaw's Rail Times 1850 F 13 0
Branch Lines series - see town names
Brecon to Neath D 43 2
Brecon to Newport D 16 6
Brecon to Newtown E 06 2
Brighton to Eastbourne A 16 1
Brighton to Worthing A 03 1
Bristol to Taunton D 03 6
Bromley South to Rochester B 23 7
Bromsgrove to Birmingham D 87 6
Bromsgrove to Gloucester D 73 9
Broxbourne to Cambridge F16 1
Brunel - A railtour D 74 6
Bude - Branch Line to B 29 9
Burnham to Evercreech Jn B 68 0
Buxton to Stockport G 32 6

C

Cambridge to Ely D 55 5
Canterbury - BLs around B 58 9
Cardiff to Dowlais (Cae Harris) E 47 5
Cardiff to Pontypridd E 95 6
Cardiff to Swansea E 42 0
Carlisle to Hawick E 85 7
Carmarthen to Fishguard E 66 6
Caterham & Tattenham Corner B251
Central & Southern Spain NG E 91 8
Chard and Yeovil - BLs a C 30 7
Charing Cross to Dartford A 75 8
Charing Cross to Orpington A 96 3
Cheddar - Branch Line to B 90 9
Cheltenham to Andover C 43 7
Cheltenham to Redditch D 81 4
Chesterfield to Lincoln G 21 0
Chester to Birkenhead F 21 5
Chester to Manchester F 51 2
Chester to Rhyl E 93 2
Chester to Warrington F 40 6
Chichester to Portsmouth A 14 7
Clacton and Walton - BLs to F 04 8
Clapham Jn to Beckenham Jn B 36 7
Cleobury Mortimer - BLs a E 18 5
Clevedon & Portishead - BLs to D180
Consett to South Shields E 57 4
Cornwall Narrow Gauge D 56 2
Corris and Vale of Rheidol E 65 9
Coventry to Leicester G 00 5
Craven Arms to Llandeilo E 35 2
Craven Arms to Wellington E 33 8
Crawley to Littlehampton A 34 5
Crewe to Manchester F 57 4
Crewe to Wigan G 12 8
Cromer - Branch Lines around C 26 0
Cromford and High Peak G 35 7
Croydon to East Grinstead B 48 0
Crystal Palace & Catford Loop B 87 1
Cyprus Narrow Gauge E 13 0

D

Darjeeling Revisited F 09 3
Darlington Leamside Newcastle E 28 4
Darlington to Newcastle D 98 2
Dartford to Sittingbourne B 34 3
Denbigh - Branch Lines around F 32 1
Derby to Chesterfield G 11 1
Derby to Stoke-on-Trent F 93 2
Derwent Valley - BL to the D 06 7
Devon Narrow Gauge E 09 3
Didcot to Banbury D 02 9
Didcot to Swindon C 84 0
Didcot to Winchester C 13 0
Diss to Norwich G 22 7
Dorset & Somerset NG D 76 0
Douglas - Laxey - Ramsey E 75 8
Douglas to Peel C 88 8
Douglas to Port Erin C 55 0
Douglas to Ramsey D 39 5
Dover to Ramsgate A 78 9
Drem to Edinburgh G 06 7
Dublin Northwards in 1950s E 31 4
Dunstable - Branch Lines to E 27 7

E

Ealing to Slough C 42 0
Eastbourne to Hastings A 27 7
East Cornwall Mineral Railways D 22 7
East Croydon to Three Bridges A 53 6
Eastern Spain Narrow Gauge E 56 7
East Grinstead - BLs to A 07 9
East Kent Light Railway A 61 1
East London - Branch Lines of C 44 4
East London Line B 80 0
East of Norwich - Branch Lines E 69 7
Effingham Junction - BLs a A 74 1
Ely to Norwich C 90 1
Enfield Town & Palace Gates D 32 6
Epsom to Horsham A 30 7
Eritrean Narrow Gauge E 38 3
Euston to Harrow & Wealdstone C 89 5
Exeter to Barnstaple B 15 2
Exeter to Newton Abbot C 49 9
Exeter to Tavistock B 69 5
Exmouth - Branch Lines to B 00 8

F

Fairford - Branch Line to A 52 9
Falmouth, Helston & St. Ives C 74 1
Fareham to Salisbury A 67 3
Faversham to Dover B 05 3
Felixstowe & Aldeburgh - BL to D 20 3
Fenchurch Street to Barking C 20 8
Festiniog - 50 yrs of enterprise C 83 3
Festiniog 1946-55 E 01 7
Festiniog in the Fifties B 68 8
Festiniog in the Sixties B 91 6
Ffestiniog in Colour 1955-82 F 25 3
Finsbury Park to Alexandra Pal C 02 8
French Metre Gauge Survivors F 88 8
Frome to Bristol B 77 0

G

Gainsborough to Sheffield G 17 3
Galashiels to Edinburgh F 52 9
Gloucester to Bristol D 35 7
Gloucester to Cardiff D 66 1
Gosport - Branch Lines around A 36 9
Greece Narrow Gauge D 72 2
Guildford to Redhill A 63 5

H

Hampshire Narrow Gauge D 36 4
Harrow to Watford D 14 2
Harwich & Hadleigh - BLs to F 02 4
Harz Revisited F 62 8
Hastings to Ashford A 37 6
Hawick to Galashiels F 36 9
Hawkhurst - Branch Line to A 66 6
Hayling - Branch Line to A 12 3
Hay-on-Wye - BL around D 92 0
Haywards Heath to Seaford A 28 4
Hemel Hempstead - BLs to D 88 3
Henley, Windsor & Marlow - BLa C77 2
Hereford to Newport D 54 8
Hertford & Hatfield - BLs a E 58 1
Hertford Loop E 71 0
Hexham to Carlisle D 75 3
Hexham to Hawick F 08 6
Hitchin to Peterborough D 07 4
Holborn Viaduct to Lewisham A 81 9
Horsham - Branch Lines to A 02 4
Hull, Hornsea and Withernsea G 27 2
Huntingdon - Branch Line to A 93 2

I

Ilford to Shenfield C 97 0
Ilfracombe - Branch Line to B 21 3
Ilkeston to Chesterfield G 26 5
Ipswich to Diss F 81 9
Ipswich to Saxmundham C 41 3
Isle of Man Railway Journey F 94 9
Isle of Wight Lines - 50 yrs C 12 3
Italy Narrow Gauge F 17 8

K

Kent Narrow Gauge C 45 1
Kettering to Nottingham F 82-6
Kidderminster to Shrewsbury E 10 9
Kingsbridge - Branch Line to C 98 7
Kings Cross to Potters Bar E 62 8
King's Lynn to Hunstanton F 58 1
Kingston & Hounslow Loops A 83 3
Kingswear - Branch Line to C 17 8

L

Lambourn - Branch Line to C 70 3
Launceston & Princetown - BLs C 19 2
Leek - Branch Line From G 01 2
Leicester to Burton F 85 7
Leicester to Nottingham G 15 9
Lewisham to Dartford A 92 5
Lincoln to Cleethorpes F 56 7
Lincoln to Doncaster G 03 6
Lines around Stamford F 98 7
Lines around Wimbledon B 75 6
Lines North of Stoke G 29 6
Liverpool Street to Chingford D 01 2
Liverpool Street to Ilford C 34 5
Llandeilo to Swansea E 46 8
London Bridge to Addiscombe B 20 6
London Bridge to East Croydon A 58 1
Longmoor - Branch Lines to A 41 3
Looe - Branch Line to C 22 2
Loughborough to Ilkeston G 24 1
Loughborough to Nottingham F 68 0
Lowestoft - BLs around E 40 6
Ludlow to Hereford E 14 7
Lydney - Branch Lines around E 26 0
Lyme Regis - Branch Line to A 45 1
Lynton - Branch Line to B 04 6

M

Machynlleth to Barmouth E 54 3
Maesteg and Tondu Lines F 06 2
Majorca & Corsica Narrow Gauge F 41 3
Mansfield to Doncaster G 23 4
March - Branch Lines around B 09 1
Market Drayton - BLs around F 67 3
Market Harborough to Newark F 86 4
Marylebone to Rickmansworth D 49 4
Melton Constable to Yarmouth Bch E031
Midhurst - Branch Lines of E 78 9
Midhurst - Branch Lines to F 00 0
Minehead - Branch Line to A 80 2
Mitcham Junction Lines B 01 5
Monmouth - Branch Lines to E 20 8
Monmouthshire Eastern Valleys D 71 5
Moretonhampstead - BL to C 27 7
Moreton-in-Marsh to Worcester D 26 5
Morpeth to Bellingham F 87 1
Mountain Ash to Neath D 80 7

N

Newark to Doncaster F 78 9
Newbury to Westbury C 66 6
Newcastle to Hexham D 69 2
Newport (IOW) - Branch Lines to A 26 0
Newquay - Branch Lines to C 71 0
Newton Abbot to Plymouth C 60 4
Newtown to Aberystwyth E 41 3
Northampton to Peterborough F 92 5
North East German NG D 44 9
Northern Alpine Narrow Gauge F 37 6
Northern France Narrow Gauge C 75 8
Northern Spain Narrow Gauge E 83 3
North London Line B 94 7
North of Birmingham F 55 0
North of Grimsby - Branch Lines G 09 8
North Woolwich - BLs around C 65 9
Nottingham to Boston F 70 3
Nottingham to Lincoln F 43 7
Nuneaton to Loughborough G 08 1

O

Ongar - Branch Line to E 05 5
Orpington to Tonbridge B 03 9
Oswestry - Branch Lines around E 60 4
Oswestry to Whitchurch E 81 9
Oxford to Bletchley D 57 9
Oxford to Moreton-in-Marsh D 15 9

P

Paddington to Ealing C 37 6
Paddington to Princes Risborough C819
Padstow - Branch Line to B 54 1
Peebles Loop G 19 7
Pembroke and Cardigan - BLs to F 29 1
Peterborough to Kings Lynn E 32 1
Peterborough to Lincoln F 89 5
Peterborough to Newark F 72 7
Plymouth - BLs around B 98 5
Plymouth to St. Austell C 63 5
Pontypool to Mountain Ash D 65 4
Pontypridd to Merthyr F 14 7
Pontypridd to Port Talbot E 86 4
Porthmadog 1954-94 - BLa B 31 2
Portmadoc 1923-46 - BLa B 13 8
Portsmouth to Southampton A 31 4
Portugal Narrow Gauge E 67 3
Potters Bar to Cambridge D 70 8
Preston to Blackpool G 16 6
Princes Risborough - BL to D 05 0
Princes Risborough to Banbury C 85 7

R

Railways to Victory C 16 1
Reading to Basingstoke B 27 5
Reading to Didcot C 79 6
Reading to Guildford A 47 5
Redhill to Ashford A 73 4
Return to Blaenau 1970-82 C 64 2
Rhyl to Bangor F 15 4
Rhymney & New Tredegar Lines E 48 2
Rickmansworth to Aylesbury D 61 6
Romania & Bulgaria NG E 23 9
Romneyrail C 32 1
Ross-on-Wye - BLs around E 30 7
Ruabon to Barmouth E 84 0
Rugby to Birmingham E 37 6
Rugby to Loughborough F 12 3
Rugby to Stafford F 07 9
Rugeley to Stoke-on-Trent F 90 1
Ryde to Ventnor A 19 2

RAIL TIMES FOR GREAT BRITAIN please request details

S

Salisbury to Westbury B 39 8
Salisbury to Yeovil B 06 0
Sardinia and Sicily Narrow Gauge F 50 5
Saxmundham to Yarmouth C 69 7
Saxony & Baltic Germany Revisited F 71 0
Saxony Narrow Gauge D 47 0
Scunthorpe to Doncaster G 34 0
Seaton & Sidmouth - BLs to A 95 6
Selsey - Branch Line to A 04 8
Sheerness - Branch Line to B 16 2
Sheffield towards Manchester G 18 0
Shenfield to Ipswich E 96 3
Shrewsbury - Branch Line to A 86 4
Shrewsbury to Chester E 70 3
Shrewsbury to Crewe F 48 2
Shrewsbury to Ludlow E 21 5
Shrewsbury to Newtown E 29 1
Sirhowy Valley Line E 12 3
Sittingbourne to Ramsgate A 90 1
Skegness & Mablethorpe - BL to F 84 0
Slough to Newbury C 56 7
South African Two-foot gauge E 51 2
Southampton to Bournemouth A 42 0
Southend & Southminster BLs E 76 5
Southern Alpine Narrow Gauge F 22 2
Southern France Narrow Gauge C 47 5
South London Line B 46 6
South Lynn to Norwich City F 03 1
Southwold - Branch Line to A 15 4
Spalding - Branch Lines around E 52
Spalding to Grimsby F 65 9 6
Stafford to Chester F 34 5
Stafford to Wellington F 59 8
St Albans to Bedford D 08 1
St. Austell to Penzance C 67 3
St. Boswell to Berwick F 44 4
Steaming Through Isle of Wight A 56
Stourbridge to Wolverhampton E 16 1
St. Pancras to Barking D 68 5
St. Pancras to Folkestone E 88 8
St. Pancras to St. Albans C 78 9
Stratford to Cheshunt F 53 6
Stratford-u-Avon to Birmingham D 77
Stratford-u-Avon to Cheltenham C 25
Sudbury - Branch Lines to F 19 2
Surrey Narrow Gauge C 87 1
Sussex Narrow Gauge C 68 0
Swaffham - Branch Lines around F 9
Swanage to 1999 - BL to A 33 8
Swanley to Ashford B 45 9
Swansea - Branch Lines around F 38
Swansea to Carmarthen E 59 8
Swindon to Bristol C 96 3
Swindon to Gloucester D 46 3
Swindon to Newport D 30 2
Swiss Narrow Gauge C 94 9

T

Talyllyn 60 E 98 7
Tamworth to Derby F 76 5
Taunton to Barnstaple B 60 2
Taunton to Exeter C 82 6
Taunton to Minehead F 39 0
Tavistock to Plymouth B 88 6
Tenterden - Branch Line to A 21 5
Three Bridges to Brighton A 35 2
Tilbury Loop C 86 4
Tiverton - BLs around C 62 8
Tivetshall to Beccles D 41 8
Tonbridge to Hastings A 44 4
Torrington - Branch Lines to B 37 4
Tourist Railways of France G 04 3
Towcester - BLs around E 39 0
Tunbridge Wells BLs A 32 1

U

Upwell - Branch Line to B 64 0
Uttoxeter to Buxton G 33 3
Uttoxeter to Macclesfield G 05 0
Uttoxetor to Buxton G 33 3

V

Victoria to Bromley South A 98 7
Victoria to East Croydon A 40 6
Vivarais Revisited E 08 6

W

Walsall Routes F 45 1
Wantage - Branch Line to D 25 8
Wareham to Swanage 50 yrs D 09 8
Waterloo to Windsor A 54 3
Waterloo to Woking A 38 3
Watford to Leighton Buzzard D 45 6
Wellingborough to Leicester F 73 4
Welshpool to Llanfair E 49 9
Wenford Bridge to Fowey C 09 3
Westbury to Bath B 55 8
Westbury to Taunton C 76 5
West Cornwall Mineral Rlys D 48 7
West Croydon to Epsom B 08 4
West German Narrow Gauge D 93 7
West London - BLs of C 50 5
West London Line B 84 8
West Wiltshire - BLs of D 12 8
Weymouth - BLs A 65 9
Willesden Jn to Richmond B 71 8
Wimbledon to Beckenham C 58 1
Wimbledon to Epsom B 62 6
Wimborne - BLs around A 97 0
Wirksworth - Branch Lines to G 10 4
Wisbech - BLs around C 01 7
Witham & Kelvedon - BLs a E 82 6
Woking to Alton A 59 8
Woking to Portsmouth A 25 3
Woking to Southampton A 55 0
Wolverhampton to Shrewsbury E 44
Wolverhampton to Stafford F 79 6
Worcester to Birmingham D 97 5
Worcester to Hereford D 38 8
Worthing to Chichester A 06 2
Wrexham to New Brighton F 47 5
Wroxham - BLs around F 31 4

Y

Yeovil - 50 yrs change C 38 3
Yeovil to Dorchester A 76 5
Yeovil to Exeter A 91 8
York to Scarborough F 23 9